MY MIGHTY HAND

I will recount the gracious deeds of the Lord ... because of all that the the Lord has done for us ... according to the abundance of his steadfast love.

    —Isaiah 63:7 (NRSV)

MY MIGHTY HAND

A Young Medical Student's Prophetic Experience and His and His Wife's Miraculous Journey from Mexico to Miami

By Richard A. Fisher, MD, MPH

Foreword by
Darrell Whiteman

RESOURCE *Publications* • Eugene, Oregon

MY MIGHTY HAND
A Young Medical Student's Prophetic Experience and His and His Wife's Miraculous Journey from Mexico to Miami

Copyright © 2024 Richard A. Fisher. All rights reserved. Except for brief quotations in critical publications or reviews, no part of this book may be reproduced in any manner without prior written permission from the publisher. Write: Permissions, Wipf and Stock Publishers, 199 W. 8th Ave., Suite 3, Eugene, OR 97401.

Resource Publications
An Imprint of Wipf and Stock Publishers
199 W. 8th Ave., Suite 3
Eugene, OR 97401

www.wipfandstock.com

PAPERBACK ISBN: 978-1-6667-8299-8
HARDCOVER ISBN: 978-1-6667-8300-1
EBOOK ISBN: 978-1-6667-8301-8

Scripture quotations marked ESV are taken from the The Holy Bible, English Standard Version, copyright © 2001 by Crossway, a publishing ministry of Good News Publishers. Used by permission. All right reserved.

Scripture quotations marked KJV are taken from the King James Version. Public domain.

Scripture quotations marked NASB are taken from the New American Standard Bible, copyright © 1960, 1962, 1963, 1968, 1971, 1972, 1973, 1975, 1977, 1995 by The Lockman Foundation. Used by permission.

Scripture quotations marked NIV are taken from the Holy Bible, New International Version, copyright © 1973, 1978, 1984, 2011 by Biblica, Inc. Used by permission of Zondervan. All rights reserved worldwide. www.Zondervan.com.

Scripture quotations marked TEV are taken from Today's English Version/Good News Translation. Copyright © 1976, 1979, 1992 by American Bible Society/Harper Collins. Used by permission. All rights reserved.

Scripture quotations marked TLB are from The Living Bible, copyright © 1971. Used by permission of Tyndale House Publishers, Inc., Carol Stream, Illinois 60188. All rights reserved.

Scripture quotations marked NRSV are from the New Revised Standard Version Bible, copyright 1989, 2009 by HarperCollins Publishers. Used by permission. All rights reserved.

Dedicated to Elaine

You stayed with me during that miraculous journey and trusted both me and the God who made all things happen according to his sovereign will. I will be forever grateful. Thanks for being with me all these years. My love for you is unceasing.

CONTENTS

Foreword by Darrell Whiteman ix
Preface xiii

PART 1

Introduction 1

1. God's Other Plans 5
2. Thinking about the Experience 15
3. The Exodus as Pattern 27
4. "And Your Young Men Shall See Visions" 33
5. Spiritual Warfare 38
6. The Kingdom of God in Miami 48
7. Whom Do You Trust? 57
8. Salvation 74
9. Seeing God 92

PART 2

Introduction: Prophetic Consciousness and Calling 101

10. Can We Wrap Our Minds around the Prophet? 103
11. My Prophetic Task 112

Epilogue 119
One Final Story 124

Bibliography 131
Index 135

FOREWORD

"Our Worldview, Science, and the Mighty Hand of God"

WHAT DO WE NORTH Americans typically do when we are confronted with what appears to be a supernatural vision? We dismiss it, because our worldview, which has been increasingly shaped by science and the Western Enlightenment paradigm for the past 300 years, doesn't make room for experiencing a vision as real and true. So, we dismiss it and explain it away, because it doesn't fit our worldview and perception of reality. Or, if we try and share it with someone else, they are likely to dismiss us. In other words, our culturally constructed perception of reality simply does not make room for such an event.

All human beings, who are created in the image of God, have a worldview, shaped by the language we speak and instilled in us at an early age. Worldviews close the distance between the world around us and the culturally agreed upon perception of that world that we carry in our minds. They also function as a lens through which we view the world and helps us distinguish what is true or false, right or wrong, possible or impossible. So, given our scientifically oriented worldview as North Americans, it is easy to dismiss a prophetic vision as simply an illusion … not to be trusted. But what if we were to have a prophetic vision, then with whom do we share the experience? Who would believe us? People might think we are crazy. We could lose respect from others.

FOREWORD

We humans strive to find meaning in our experiences of life. This is one of the functions of our worldview, and down through time and across the planet today, the worldviews of human beings have varied, sometimes dramatically so. For example, in the worldviews of people in the non-Western Majority World, where the natural and supernatural world are not so sharply divided, but rather form a seamless whole between the unseen world and the visible world, visions are not so unusual. They occur and are often trusted. For example, in the past some Native Americans pursued a vision quest. In the Islamic world today, many Muslims are experiencing visions of Jesus (who they call "Isa") appearing to them in their dreams, which leads them to become followers of Jesus.

Melanesian people, with whom I have lived in the Solomon Islands and Papua New Guinea, often receive messages from God in their dreams. So, for example, if they follow the advice given to them in a dream, and everything turns out as they expected, it confirms for them that dreams are a reliable way to receive a message from God. But what happens if they follow the advice they believe God gave them, and it does *not* turn out right. How do they explain it then? We, in the West, with our Enlightenment and scientific worldview, would quickly conclude, "See, you can't trust advice given in dreams and visions!" But a Melanesian would not draw that conclusion. To the contrary, he or she would conclude they must go back and dream that dream again, because they must not have heard God's voice clearly the first time.

In the pages that follow you are going to be introduced to a young medical student, trained in science, and a person of deep biblical faith, who had an encounter with God in which God told him what was going to happen in the near future. How would he make sense out of this experience? Was it true? Was it an illusion? Was it just a dream? Was it simply a coincidence that what he thought God showed him and told him, in fact actually came true? You'll be captivated by this story. Dr. Fisher has waited forty years before he was ready to publicly publish the experience of his vision as a message from God. Why wait so long? For starters, most

FOREWORD

Americans would question if this really happened. Some skeptics would conclude that it was just a coincidence, nothing more.

So, what can we learn from his remarkable story? In 1 John 4:1, John instructs believers to "test the spirits" when something seems out of the ordinary, is unusual, and perhaps doesn't make sense in terms of their worldview and assumptions about reality. This is exactly what Dr. Fisher has done—he has tested his experience against the yardstick of Scripture. Did it measure up? You'll discover the answer to that question as you read this book and find out.

Dr. Fisher took seriously the notion of testing the spirits and searching the Scriptures to understand his prophetic vision. As a biblically informed lay person, he looked for patterns, symbols, types, and metaphors in the Bible, all held together by a meta-narrative or story-line that holds the whole of Scripture together, from Genesis to Revelation. As he tells his story, we'll be introduced to lessons of obedience from Abraham and Isaiah. We'll discover that the cultural mandate for human beings to have dominion over the earth does not mean to fight it and destroy it. Western Christians owe their view of a hostile nature more to the Greeks and their dualistic thinking, that separated the supernatural world from the natural world, than they do to the story of the Bible that encourages us to be stewards of the land and engage in creation care.

Dr. Fisher reminds us that God's plan for salvation, is much more than a "ticket to get into heaven," but rather is the salvation and renewal of the entire universe as well as our planet earth. In other words, God's salvation is for the entire cosmos, our planet, our communities, and not just for individuals. In the following pages we'll explore different models of spiritual warfare, and note the role of prophets in the Old Testament, especially Amos who has something to teach us today, especially in how to confront evil and hypocrisy in the church. Dr. Fisher shares his painful experience of drawing on the model of Amos in confronting fraudulent behavior and hypocrisy in the church.

The story of *My Mighty Hand* told by a medical doctor who loves Jesus and believes the Bible to be true, will encourage and

FOREWORD

inspire you to see where God is at work in your own spiritual pilgrimage. I invite you to read this timely and important work with an open mind, and be prepared to have your own worldview challenged in ways you may not have expected.

Darrell Whiteman
16 July 2024
Gig Harbor, Washington

PREFACE

FORTY YEARS CAN BE a long time to wait, especially to write a book about a personal experience. But over four decades ago God came to me in two prophetic visions that predicted future events. As a direct result of the visions, my wife, Elaine, and I left one country and went to another. We left on faith, trusting that God would be faithful to his promise. Sounds a bit like like Abram and Sarai, doesn't it? We were young at the time. (I was thirty-two and Elaine twenty-six.) I doubt that I fully comprehended in any manner what God had done for us. So, as I have been reflecting on my forty-year pilgrimage of trying to understand the significance of this experience and to frame it within a biblical understanding, I'll be looking at it through the lens of several biblical themes.

Predictive prophecy does not happen often to North American believers, but it happened to us; and it has changed me profoundly. Who wouldn't be transformed when the Creator and Lord of the universe stoops down and speaks to you and tells you future events? How could it not shake you to your very core—when you see those predictions unfold before your very eyes?

In order to figure out what exactly God did through this prophetic experience, I have been forever shaped by Scripture. God, in his providence, has also led me to some of the best in biblical scholarship. Some of my core beliefs have been challenged and changed.[1] Had it not been for this prophetic walk, I don't believe I

---

1. The prophetic experience of four decades ago has led to profound changes in my thinking and my Christian worldview by searching God's Word and

would have the love for God's Word that I now have. Like a good Berean, I have "received the word with all eagerness, examining the Scriptures daily to see if these things were so." (Acts 17:11b ESV). God has taught me much (Isa 54:13; John 6:45).

In the theology of Deuteronomy, remembering and forgetting are fundamental concepts. Listen to what it says to us: "Take care lest you forget the Lord your God by not keeping his commandments and his rules and his statutes, which I command you today, . . . and you forget the Lord your God, who brought you out of the land of Egypt, . . . who led you through the great and terrifying wilderness, . . . You shall remember the Lord your God . . . (Deut 8:11–18a ESV).

God wants us to recall his unique acts so that our lives will be in keeping with his holy character. If we don't reflect God's touch in our lives, we really have not understood what that touch of God means. We have not truly remembered what God has done for us. Remembering God's acts in the past is not for the sake of nostalgia but for the sake of spiritual renewal (Ps 9:1–2).

I am not a professional theologian or in the academic community. Nevertheless, I have always had a religious and theological bent. (When I was a teenager, my mother complained that I was reading theology books that were "too deep." I was going to be "too heavenly minded to be of any earthly good." Well, I didn't have my "head in the clouds," nor did I buy her criticism, because I also loved sports and other "normal" activities. Besides, being a medical doctor does some earthly good, I would think.)

I do write with some theological reflection. Although not everyone gets all "warm and toasty" over theology, I see no other way to approach the experience God gave us. Everyone has a theology—even atheists. The question is whether we will be responsible or not in thinking about God. I see a beauty in theological activity; what could be more worthwhile than thinking about God—his words and works? I could give you textbook definitions

---

applying it to many areas of my life untouched before the experience. Before I began thinking about God's mighty deed, it was more or less a raw experience.

of theology—most of them long and boring—but for me theology is simply a personal quest to understand and know God better.

I see writing this book as an act of worship. The trained theologian or pastor may or may not find it useful—or even correct on some theological points. The tone is, for the most part, serious, because what God did for Elaine and me was a numinous experience, not to be treated with any sense of levity.

I have two basic reasons in writing this book: First, to glorify God. Second, there is a serious need among believers to be aware that God is not silent and is still active, even in miraculous ways, in the lives of his people. J. P. Moreland, in *Kingdom Triangle*,[2] argues that we as believers get mistaken impressions that God is relatively absent in today's world because we lack awareness of the incredible things he is doing in the lives of other Christians.

I would hope that this story of God's gracious intervention in the lives of two young believers in a foreign country would open others to God's supernatural intervention today. Gary Habermas, in a review of Moreland's book, thinks that we are like those who witness the supernatural, but attribute it "to thunder" (John 12:29).[3]

Moreland thinks that we, as believers, need to take appropriate yearly risks and put ourselves in situations in which "God must show up."[4] To be sure, this book is about that—taking risks and "burning bridges." It's about stepping out in faith based on the promises of God.

My prayer is that sharing this testimony of believers stepping out in faith and obedience to God will change your life.

---

2. Moreland, *Kingdom Triangle*, 134–35.
3. Habermas, *Philosophia Christi*, 215–23.
4. Moreland, *Kingdom Triangle*, 134.

PART 1

INTRODUCTION

WE ALL HAVE STORIES. You have one. God has one, too—it's recorded in the Bible as redemptive history. It's the grand narrative of salvation from Eden to the new Jerusalem; one wrought by the new Adam, our Lord Jesus Christ.

My wife, Elaine, and I also have a story—one that happened over forty years ago. Like everyone's, ours is unique. You may wonder why I've waited so long to tell ours . . . a very good question.

Our experience occurred when I was a medical student in Guadalajara, Mexico, and it involved a surprising work of the Holy Spirit. It required our trust in God, a willingness to take bridge-burning risks, and an Abraham-like obedience to a promise of God that he made about a future event.

However, let me give you a little background about ourselves and how we wound up in Mexico. After five years of military service in Germany in the Air Force during the Vietnam War era, I enrolled in premed studies at Purdue University in my hometown of Fort Wayne, Indiana. Before enlisting in the Air Force I had completed three years of college. But, with the contentious Vietnam War escalating, the military draft hanging over my head, and America in political and social turmoil, I was, quite frankly, unsettled—like a ship without a rudder. My academic record was, therefore, less than stellar. So, in 1969 I started my tour of duty in Germany.

INTRODUCTION TO PART 1

While serving in Germany I had a military buddy, Wayne, from Nebraska. One evening while he was telling me about his ill mother, I had a lightbulb moment. I *knew* I wanted to be a medical doctor. (More accurately, I believe God wanted me to go into medicine.) So, for the two remaining years or so on my tour I spent virtually all my evenings at the military library in Germany devouring every biology and chemistry textbook or anything else that would prepare me for premed studies. I think my efforts paid off because once at Purdue University, I had competitive grades.

It was during my Purdue years that an attractive young lady caught my eye: Elaine. She was an "MK," a missionary kid, whose parents were back from the then-named Zaïre on furlough. They happened to live in a house next to my parents, where I was staying. This made it easy for Elaine and me to get to know each other. (Really, who needs online dating when God's plans are so perfect!)

I had aspirations to be a missionary (I had previously gone to Jamaica in the late 60s prior to enlisting in the military to visit the newly founded Jamaica Theological Seminary and visit missionaries in the Dominican Republic), so Elaine and I had much in common. But I knew she was a believer, the most important thing to me. After a courtship of about eighteen months, we were married in Fort Wayne in August 1976, after I had graduated from Purdue University in June the same year.

Prior to that, however, I had applied to three medical schools in the Midwest, including Indiana University School of Medicine. I was rejected by all three. As things would have it, however, Elaine's father was a well-known and well-connected missionary in the Midwest and knew several influential Christian doctors in Indiana. One of them sat on the admissions committee at the School of Medicine at Indiana University, so through this connection I was reinstated as a full applicant, with the argument that my pre-military grades were not a true reflection of my academic abilities. But the admission committee didn't buy my argument and rejected my application a second time. I was very disappointed—so took a position as a pharmaceutical representative, which was my job when we were married.

INTRODUCTION TO PART 1

Although I felt fairly well situated as a pharmaceutical salesman—making sales calls on physicians—I knew something was missing. What about that lightbulb experience when I was in Germany? One eventful day I met a family doctor, John, in rural Indiana who had graduated from medical school at Guadalajara, Mexico, and who encouraged me to at least consider the foreign medical school option. Elaine and I became friends with John and his wife, Debbie, both of whom were believers. They got us excited about a wonderful house church that met in Guadalajara. So, Elaine and I prayed about it and decided to take the risk. I quit my job, paid the hefty enrollment fee, and we moved to Mexico.

The medical school experience in Mexico was frustrating because all classes were in Spanish—not exactly a strength of mine. But I was at least getting a medical education. I should mention that most of us American medical students were there because we had been rejected by the American medical school system.

We all react to rejection in different ways.[1] Some of us accepted the foreign medical school option and were resigned to graduating from Guadalajara. Others reacted with extra motivation and were focused on transferring to an American medical school. Some were obsessed with transfer to an American medical school. The golden ticket for transfer, however, was Part 1 of the National Board of Medical Examiners. You had to do well on that exam.

My position was probably one of moderation; I certainly wanted to transfer. (Transfer to an American medical school would have been a dream come true.) However, Elaine and I found the house church in Guadalajara to be wonderfully spiritually nourishing. It was hosted by a missionary couple from Dallas, J. B. and Mildred, a godly Pentecostal couple. To top it off, Guadalajara was a lovely city, with beautiful flora and a temperate year-round climate—almost edenic—so leaving would not have been easy.

However, God had other plans.

---

1. Athletes who are rejected in some manner may react with extra motivation. I find it hard to believe that Michael Jordan, Tom Brady, and Stephen Curry, all of whom were overlooked in some way in their athletic careers, didn't want to prove their detractors wrong. All three have had transcendent careers in their respective sports.

1

GOD'S OTHER PLANS

> To the glory of the most high God, and that my neighbor may be benefitted thereby.
> —Johann Sebastian Bach, title page of *Orgelbuechlein*

ONE EVENING, AS ELAINE and I were in our apartment in Guadalajara singing and praising the Lord, I felt an overwhelming feeling that I needed to be alone. This was at a time in our lives when we were extremely close to the Lord. We were constantly, it seems, engaging in praise to the triune God. Whenever I was not in class at the medical school at Guadalajara, studying, or other routine things, my mind was focused on the Lord Jesus. They were spiritually heady times for us.

Anyway, I went into my study, sat down in the Barcalounger that my parents had given to us as a wedding present, closed my eyes, and received a prophetic word from the Lord in the form of a vision. I was, like Jack Deere, "surprised by the voice of God."[1] I saw the voice of the Lord, who revealed two things: I was going to transfer to the University of Miami, and Dan Shover (a Christian friend and classmate) was going to suffer persecution. Words come up a bit short in describing how Elaine and I felt at

---

1. Deere, *Surprised by the Voice of God*. This is a wonderful book describing the deeply personal ways God can speak to us today. Deere speaks from personal experience and as a trained theologian. Highly recommended.

that time because we had experienced the transcendent. The Lord had spoken.[2]

A few nights later, Dan came to our apartment on his motorcycle. He had just come from a local Mexican prison, where he had been witnessing to inmates. Someone obviously didn't appreciate Dan's witness or inmates coming to Christ, so he threatened Dan with a handgun to stop witnessing at the prison. Dan was a bit shaken by the incident, but when he learned that the Lord had told me days earlier that he would suffer for Christ, we were filled with a sense of God's presence and protection.

The following week the voice of the Lord came to me a second time in a vision. Again, this was preceded by an intense feeling of wanting to be alone. This time, however, God addressed me personally and said, "My son, you will transfer to Miami this summer by my mighty hand." In the first vision, God revealed *what* would

---

2. What I "saw" were words in a sequence of white light (even though my eyes were closed) going horizontally, accompanied by a voice that bypassed my own sense of hearing. They were not my thoughts because they bypassed my cognition. Deere, *Surprised by the Voice of God*, 130–41, comments on the different ways that God can speak to us. He says that God certainly can and has spoken through an audible voice, although he admits he has never experienced God in this way. The way Deere has experienced the supernatural voice of God is via an internal voice . . . not an audible voice that anyone else could hear, but the words of God in complete sentences.

This is what I experienced . . . the voice of God, speaking in complete sentences, addressing me with a kind tone. I experienced a vision, not some "still, small voice" in my heart. Still, small voices don't make predictions of the future. My experience was not a hallucination or a seizure, nor hocus-pocus, none of which can predict the future. It was God's free sovereign pleasure to speak to me this way. I knew the thoughts were not my own because they bypassed my own volition.

I don't know what the Old Testament prophet Amos experienced, but he records in Amos 1:1 (ESV) that he "saw" words concerning Israel. In addition, Isaiah "saw" the prophetic words concerning Judah and Jerusalem (Isa 2:1 ESV). So, seeing the voice of God is thoroughly biblical. Hamilton, *With the Clouds of Heaven*, 113, mentions that the "wording of Daniel 9:23 indicates that a revelatory word . . . is tantamount to beholding vision" and references Goldingay and Collins, who both indicate that the word and vision are equivalent. (Collins, *Daniel*, 352; Goldingay, *Daniel*, 228.)

happen; now he was revealing *when* and *how*. The Lord was now specifying a time and a manner.[3,4]

So, I disenrolled from medical school at Guadalajara. Elaine and I then moved to Daytona Beach, Florida, where her parents, who were missionaries to Zaïre (now the Democratic Republic of the Congo) and back on furlough, had a home. I did well on my interviews at the University of Miami School of Medicine and received good scores on Part 1 of the NBME (National Board of Medical Examiners), so we were upbeat. After all, had not the all-knowing and all-powerful God predicted the transfer?

At the end of July 1979, I was telephoning the medical school at Miami weekly to get updates on transfer decisions. Invariably, I was told, "no decisions yet," but was advised that the admissions committee was to decide on transfers the second week of August. So, in a step of faith, Elaine and I decided to drive to Fort Wayne, Indiana, where we had been married three years earlier, to pick up the rest of our possessions and bring them back to Florida.

In my mid-60s Chevy van, we were accompanied by Elaine's mother and grandmother in their vehicle. What a trip! My van

---

3. It's amazing that it's taken me over forty years to catch on (I guess I'm a slow learner.) to the significance of the *white* light voice/visions that I experienced in Guadalajara in 1979. They could have been multicolored lights like on a Christmas tree . . . but they weren't. As I was studying John's Revelation, 19:11–21, describing the last apocalyptic battle and triumph of Christ, I noticed he comes riding on a *white* horse. In addition, the armies of heaven are arrayed in fine linen, *white* and pure, and following him on *white* horses. Then in 20:11 God is seated on a great *white* throne to judge all mankind. So, it seems to me that in Revelation, at least, *white* is a symbol of God's holiness and purity and makes my experience all the more amazing and validating.

4. Although I experienced the voice of God in the form of a vision, Scripture is full of humans receiving revelation from God, much of it enscripturated in canonical form. Such revelation is massive condescension on God's part. It goes without saying that the incarnation of Jesus Christ was the ultimate condescension of the triune God, but for God to reveal himself in human language is itself an accommodation that God is willing to make. I don't believe God can be known by us in his essence. In other words, we as humans cannot penetrate the essence or being of God as God.

Reformed theologian Douglas Kelly summarizes this position of the transcendent inscrutability of God as profoundly biblical. See Kelly, *Systematic Theology*, 1:302–03.

broke down so many times that we were beginning to think that making the trip was a mistake. On a humorous note, Elaine's grandmother, who was in her mid-80s, in a moment of frustration scolded me and said, " You shoulda bought a Ford, and then we wouldn't always be breaking down!"

Well, maybe I "shoulda bought a Ford," but God came through. In Adel, Georgia, where we were forced to stop for repairs because of a faulty radiator fan clutch, I was really happy to find the part at Brook's NAPA Auto Parts early Saturday afternoon. I thought we were in business until I discovered that I had bought the wrong-sized part. I went back to the parts store, but it had closed for the weekend. Our frustration only grew when we drove around Adel for what seemed like an eternity in the other vehicle (a Ford!), unable to find a decent restaurant.

We got lost but happened to drive into the parking lot of the Adel Church of God to turn around to find our way back to our motel—but noticed a yellow church bus. As we drove up to it, we saw two men inside, apparently making repairs. As Elaine's mother approached the men to ask for directions (this was before GPS), I noticed a black Chevy El Camino parked at the side of the bus. On the side of the El Camino was the lettering "Brook's NAPA Auto Parts." We could not believe our eyes! One of the men worked at the auto parts store where I had just purchased the wrong part! He reopened the store, exchanged the part, and told me how God had delivered him from alcoholism. More breakdowns on the trip could not dampen our sense of being in God's everlasting arms.

After we returned to Daytona Beach, I telephoned the medical school the second week of August, which was the week I was told the admissions committee was to decide on transfers. However, I was informed that transfer decisions had been made the *first week* of August and that I had not been accepted. I received my denial letter, dated August 8. Elaine and I were confused and devastated, so we did the only thing we knew to do—we went to God in prayer.

We were led by the Lord to call Bill Cooper, then an ob-gyn resident at Georgia Baptist Hospital in Atlanta. Bill had been a medical student at Guadalajara who had been unjustly expelled from school. Elaine and I had been impressed by Bill's testimony, which he had given previously in the home meetings at Guadalajara. Walking by faith, Bill was admitted to George Washington University School of Medicine the very same day a student happened to drop out of classes.

Our prayers were not in vain—God used Bill in a miraculous way. After explaining our situation to him, he told us to "claim" my position in the medical school. He had been reading 1 Samuel 30:1–8, where David was in a desperate situation and in danger of being stoned by his own people. The Amalekites had plundered the town of Ziklag and carried off the wives, sons, and daughters of Israel, including David's two wives. When David inquired of the Lord, his answer was to "pursue" the enemy. In addition to this scriptural confirmation, the Lord spoke directly through Bill by saying, "Do not waver in faith, and do not believe this evil report."

"Pursuing the enemy," Elaine and I started driving to Miami from Daytona Beach around midnight and arrived at the School of Medicine about six o'clock in the morning, August 10. (We took Elaine's sister's car—a Ford, no less! I wasn't putting much trust in my old van anymore after all the previous breakdowns. Perhaps my faith in God was waning. Anyway, we made it to Miami. Unfortunately, however, her Mustang was vandalized and the CB radio stolen while we were in Miami.)

We explained our situation to various deans, including the assistant to the dean of the medical school. She rebuked me for my "stupidity" because I hadn't gone back to Guadalajara after being denied transfer to Miami. But she referred us to an associate dean, Dr. Bragg, who was very kind and sympathetic to our situation. There was one problem: the dean we needed to talk to, Barbara Binns, was in London on vacation until the first week of September, when classes were to begin for second-year students. (God's timing is faultless because Friday was the only day of the week Dr. Bragg met with students in his office.)

So, Elaine and I did an outrageous thing—we moved to Miami! I will never forget the response of Elaine's mother when we told her we were moving to Miami—she said, "You're doing what!?" However, knowing that God would be faithful to his promise, we moved all of our furniture (which wasn't a lot) into a house in Miami Springs. We signed a rental agreement and paid the deposit even though there were no openings in the second-year class. We stayed in touch with the medical school, especially to know when Ms. Binns was to return. I encountered one administrative assistant who was consistently hostile and intimidating. She informed me there were "no openings" in the second-year class and none would open up. She told me to "give up." We were discouraged but knew Satan was trying to make us abandon our trust in God's promise. In that hour, we were led to the Word of God to sustain and encourage us. First Peter 3:14 states, "But even if you should suffer for the sake of righteousness, you are blessed. And do not fear their intimidation and do not be troubled" (NASB).

The week before classes were to begin, I was led to Numbers 13. Moses had sent twelve spies into Caanan to figure out how strong the inhabitants were. Ten spies brought back discouraging information—the people of Caanan were giants and their cities fortified. They said, "We be not able to go up against the people; for they are stronger than we. And they brought up an *evil report* of the land which they had searched . . ." (vv. 31b–32a KJV, italics added).Suddenly, it dawned on me that the "evil report" that Bill Cooper alluded to was denial letter, the intimidation, the rebuke—all of Satan's attempts to get Elaine and me to give up and fail to believe the promise of God.

Maybe God felt we needed more scriptural confirmation, because it kept coming. God led Elaine to Isaiah 46:9–10. Listen to this precious promise: ". . . I clearly told you what was going to happen in the future. For I am God—I only—and there is no other like me who can tell you what is going to happen. All I say will come to pass, for I do whatever I wish" (TLB).

If that weren't enough, God showed me 1 Peter 5:6–9, a wonderful source of strength: "Humble yourselves, therefore, under the mighty hand of God, that he may exalt you at the proper time . . . your adversary, the devil, prowls about like a roaring lion seeking someone to devour. But resist him, firm in your faith" (TEV). Our faith was being completed and perfected by our works. No giants in the land were going to be able to hinder what God had spoken.

The weekend before classes at Miami were to begin was Labor Day weekend, so Elaine and I spent it with her family in Daytona Beach. We started back to Miami on Sunday, September 2, but ran into a little bad weather—Hurricane David! As we stopped for gas at Fort Pierce along the Florida Turnpike, a wild-looking, unkempt female who appeared to be in her thirties came up to me to announce that Miami had been destroyed by the hurricane and we needed to turn back. Elaine and I looked at each other and smiled because we knew we were hearing an "evil report." If we had heeded her lie, we would not have arrived at Miami at all. As it turned out, the hurricane, which was initially projected to make landfall at Miami, made a northward turn up the East Coast instead. So, if we had turned back, it would have been difficult, if not impossible, to travel south during the next few days. Anyway, Hurricane David went north—and we went south, to our home in Miami Springs, where we waited for Labor Day weekend to end.

A Bible verse that is especially dear to us is 2 Chronicles 20:15-17, which was given to us that Labor Day weekend. It says, "... This is what the Lord says to you: 'Do not fear or be dismayed ... for the battle is not yours but God's. Tomorrow, go down against them ... You need not fight in this battle; station yourself, stand and see the salvation of the Lord on your behalf ... Do not fear or be dismayed; tomorrow go out to face them, for the Lord is with you'" (NASB).

So, on Tuesday, September 4, with our faith in God's promise soaring, we did as God told us. We stationed ourselves ... in Barbara Binns' office! She had returned from London and was busy, but she agreed to see us. I told her I was "ready to begin classes!" I also informed her I was claiming my position in the second-year class. I don't know what she was really thinking, but she politely told me that transfer was "an impossibility" because there were no openings. However, she graciously invited us to return the following day to discuss things further. The next day, Ms. Binns had learned that a second-year student had taken a leave of absence the previous day! Given this turn of events, she had to discuss the matter with various medical school deans and the admissions committee and said she would me call the next day. Elaine and I had hearts bursting with joy and praise for the God who is true to his promises.

I will never forget the words of Ms. Binns, who called me the next morning around nine o'clock to inform me that I had been accepted into the second-year class. She matter-of-factly stated, "The powers that be are with you; you have been accepted into the second-year class." I'll never know for sure, but my impression at that time was that her wording may have been an implicit acknowledgement that our being in just the right place at just the right time was more than mere chance—that there was a higher power behind all this. She certainly could have used a more standard phrase for my acceptance, i.e., the admissions committee, but she didn't. I received my letter of acceptance dated September 6, 1979, which was the *good report*, one that was the result of a God who is faithful to keep his word and is to be praised forever!

FIGURE 1

UNIVERSITY OF MIAMI
MIAMI, FLORIDA 33101

ADMISSIONS
SCHOOL OF MEDICINE
P. O. BOX 016159

August 8, 1979

Mr. Richard A. Fisher
921 Sandcrest Drive
Port Orange, Florida 32019

Dear Mr. Fisher:

The Committee on Admissions reviewed your application for transfer to the University of Miami School of Medicine for 1979. We are sorry to inform you that it was the decision of the Committee that it cannot offer you an opportunity to enter at that time.

We thank you for your interest in the University of Miami School of Medicine and wish you luck in the future.

Sincerely yours,

Barbara Binns (Miss)
Associate Dean for
Admissions

BB/pr

A private, independent, international university
An equal opportunity/affirmative action employer

My letter of denial from the University of Miami School of Medicine, dated August 8, 1979.

MY MIGHTY HAND

FIGURE 2

```
                    UNIVERSITY OF MIAMI
                      MIAMI, FLORIDA 33101

    ADMISSIONS
  SCHOOL OF MEDICINE
    P. O. BOX 016159                       September 6, 1979
```

Mr. Richard A. Fisher
380 Payne Drive
Miami Springs, Florida

Dear Mr. Fisher:

    This is to advise you that you have been accepted into the Second Year class at the University of Miami School of Medicine which will begin this month. We need three affidavits of residency and a Health Form (forms enclosed) to complete your file as soon as possible.

    Please notify my office by letter of your acceptance or rejection of this offer immediately.

    We shall be looking forward to your enrollment as one of our students. If you desire further information, please contact us.

                              Sincerely yours,

                              Barbara Binns (Miss)
                              Associate Dean for
                              Admissions

Encls.

BB/pr

A private, independent, international university
An equal opportunity/affirmative action employer

My letter of acceptance from the University of Miami School of Medicine, dated September 6, 1979

2

THINKING ABOUT THE EXPERIENCE

Allow me to explain the general drift of where we're going in this book. In this chapter, I'll try to accomplish three things:

First, our testimony, no matter how astonishing or miraculous, needs to be understood in light of God's Word. Secondly, I will briefly discuss how this experience has heightened my understanding of how God uses human language in communicating with us—something that never dawned on me previously. This is a direct result of God talking to me through visions four decades ago in human language—in clear English sentences.

Lastly, I will address God's use of patterns in his interactions with us. More explicitly, the use of biblical patterns by God and the words God chose to use when he addressed me four decades ago are discussed. In the rest of the book, I will bring in and develop specific biblical themes that explain our experience, along with the many things God has taught me over the past four decades.

Before I get into the nitty-gritty, I need to state that since God's "mighty hand" was powerfully involved in our wondrous experience from Guadalajara to Miami, it's legitimate to wonder why I've waited four decades to bringing this testimony "out of the wilderness." Forty years or so is a long time to keep an experience like this under wraps. I'm sure we all would agree God wants his mighty deeds brought into the church through personal testimony to glorify himself and edify believers. O. Palmer Robertson tells us that first-person testimony goes back to the earliest days of Israel, when God's people came forward publicly at the end of a long pilgrimage to benefit future generations after entering the promised land.[1]

In light of this, it wasn't until my own long pilgrimage of searching the Bible and understanding certain scriptural truths that I figured out what God had done four decades ago. I could not have shared this experience in a worthy manner without years of searching and understanding.

GOD'S DEEDS EXPLAINED BY HIS WORDS

Naively, I had always thought that our experience spoke for itself—that it best stood on its own as an example of God's mighty power. We believers often give our testimonies in church, often of Jesus saving us of from our sins. This is fine. But our Guadalajara-to-Miami experience is best understood (by myself and others) when filtered through the lens of Scripture—like looking through a prism that sheds different colors of light on things. One reason for this is because what happened to us is so unusual—at least in Western culture—and the story multilayered that it needs—and almost begs—to be explained by the written Word.

George Eldon Ladd is helpful.[2] He states that God's mighty deeds are explained by his Word—what he calls a "deed-word"

---

1. Robertson states, "According to the record of Deuteronomy, first-person testimony with a carefully structured format was legislated as a regular ritual for Israel . . . After entering the land of promise, the individual Israelite was to bring the first fruits of the land to a divinely designated dwelling place of God's name . . . and declare his personal testimony," which was quite extensive (Deut 26:3–11). The testimony was public, given in first-person singular, and given at the *end of a long pilgrimage through life* (italics added) and for future generations. Robertson is writing from the perspective from the book of Ecclesiastes, but he states that repeatedly across the generations of redemptive history, God's people come forward. Robertson, *Christ of Wisdom*, 217–21.

2. Ladd, *New Testament and Criticism*.

pattern. Ladd argues that God's works do not speak for themselves, but God gives a divine word of interpretation, so that his mighty acts cannot be understood apart from the divine word. This, according to Ladd, is the basic reality of biblical revelation. In other words, this is how God works.[3] So, if this is how God works, then our experience of God's mighty hand would be best explained by examining the Bible, which is what I try to demonstrate in this book.

HOW I READ THE BIBLE DIFFERENTLY

However, by reading and studying God's Word to understand our experience, I have developed an ever-deepening love for his Word! The psalmist says it best:

> the precepts of the Lord are right, rejoicing the heart . . .
> More to be desired are they than gold, even much fine gold; sweeter also than honey and . . . the honeycomb.
> (Ps 19:8a–10 ESV)

But I also read it differently than, say, twenty or thirty years ago. Let me elaborate a bit.

No longer do I read the Bible mainly like a divinely inspired philosophy book chock-full of propositional truths about God, Christ, etc. Clearly, I'm not denying that there are propositional or

---

3. Ladd states: "At this point we are confronted by the central feature of the biblical truth of revelation and of the role of the Bible in this divine self-revelation: God has revealed Himself to men not only in words, but first of all in acts, in deeds, in historical events." Ladd goes on to say that the exodus event was divine self-revelation through mighty acts—his mighty deeds. This act of God was not a bare event of divine salvation. "God's works did not speak for themselves; along with the event, He gave a divine word of interpretation. God acted, and God spoke; and his word explained the event." Ladd believes this is the divine mode of revelation: "the revealing acts of God in history, accompanied by the interpreting prophetic word which explains the divine source and character of the divine acts. Deeds—words; God acts—God speaks; and the words explain the deeds." Ladd thinks both acts and words belong together to form an inseparable unity and provide the basic structure of the biblical reality of revelation. Ladd, *New Testament and Criticism*, 26–27.

factual statements of divinely inspired truth in the Bible. There are, and they are essential to our faith.[4]

But because I had previously wanted *only* the "hard facts" of God's Word, I was missing its story line. In other words, I was missing the narrative structure of God's Word—of how it's actually put together.

SYMBOLISM AND METAPHORS—HOW GOD SPEAKS TO US

James Hamilton, in his delightful book *What Is Biblical Theology?*, argues that if we don't understand Scripture's symbolism (figurative language), we will not understand fully the biblical authors' message.[5] Before I go further, let's take a time-out. Don't let the word "symbolism" put you off. It's an extremely important concept if we want to understand the Bible God gave us.[6]

A couple of modern-day examples will help. Simply defined, a symbol is something that stands for something else. For example, we all know that that the donkey (among other things) is a symbol of the Democratic Party and the elephant the Republican Party. "Bullish" vs. "bearish" markets are symbols describing how the stock markets are performing. We know these things because they are a part of the cultural air we breathe. These symbols form a tiny part of what is called our "symbolic universe," which is made of countless other symbols that we most likely are not conscious of but use to explain and make sense of the world.

---

4. Certainly Scripture contains revealed propositional truth about God, Jesus Christ, the Holy Spirit, his grand redemptive plan, etc. However, the Bible also has a rich and complex symbolic universe, which I had missed for years.

5. Hamilton, *What Is Biblical Theology?*, 61–65. This is a great readable book to introduce someone to the beauty of biblical theology.

6. Although symbolic language can have precise and technical definitions, and include metaphors, similes, metonymy, synecdoche, I will be less restrictive and will include all these under the umbrella of figurative language, which I will assume is synonymous with symbolic language. Scholarship, however, would make many technical distinctions.

The Bible is chock-full of symbols. Jesus often used symbols/metaphors to convey heavenly truths. Who of us does not know of Jesus' parables meant to teach us spiritual truths? He frequently referred to himself in earthly metaphors such as bread, water, a shepherd, and a vine to reveal his identity.

But Hamilton is right: if we don't understand biblical imagery, we get lost in Scripture. It's easy to do because it's as if we live on a different planet than the biblical writers. Who of us makes bloody sacrifices of bulls? What about all those restrictive laws? Instructions to treat slaves well? After all, we live in the digital age with freedom and rights. So, many symbols and figurative language used in the Bible sound outright weird to us.

Let me indulge in more examples. How many of us would know what the the "stump of Jesse" (Isa 11:10a ESV) refers to? Some of us might. However, what about such verses as Ezekiel 5:10a (ESV), which says, "Therefore fathers shall eat their sons in your midst, and sons shall eat their fathers. And I will execute judgments on you . . ."? Or what about Hosea 13:16b (ESV): ". . . their little ones shall be dashed in pieces, and their pregnant women ripped open"?[7] Very difficult verses for us moderns.

LANGUAGE IN GOD'S WORD

Moving on, as I have had to wrestle with the idea of metaphor and symbolism used by God himself in our Guadalajara experience, I've had to think about human language in general and how it's used in the Bible. In other words, I've had to think about how God reveals himself to us through human language. Now, I am not a philosopher of language—not even in the same ballpark. However, I do understand that human language is complex and the issues around it debated by those much smarter than I am. I find the position in a landmark book by Lakoff and Johnson to be convincing:

---

7. Sandy, *Plowshares & Pruning Hooks*, 79. These examples come from Sandy's book, which is a wonderful place to start to understand the role of language in the Bible, especially in the prophets.

> Metaphor is for most people . . . a matter of extraordinary rather than ordinary language . . . a matter of words rather than thought or action. For this reason, most people think they can get along perfectly well without metaphor. *We have found, on the contrary, that metaphor is pervasive in everyday life* (italics added), not just in language but in thought and action. Our ordinary conceptual system, in terms of which we both think and act, is fundamentally metaphorical in nature . . . the way we think, what we experience and what we do every day is very much a matter of metaphor.[8]

What I believe they are saying is that although we are not consciously aware of it, in most of the little things we do every day, metaphors (understanding one thing in terms of another) structure how we perceive and think, and what we do.[9] Metaphors are the air we breathe. They help us make sense of the world.

If you find it hard to wrap your mind around this, let me give you a thought experiment: try to think about God without the use of metaphors or figurative language. It's hard—if not impossible—to think about him in totally abstract terms. That's why God reveals himself to us in creaturely terms—in his mighty deeds, his names, his attributes.

God reveals himself to us as a man—in *anthropomorphic* terms—even though he is a spirit (John 4:24). He chooses to tell about himself through the metaphoric use of human anatomy (arm, hand, eye, ears). We know him and pray to him as God our Father, using our human concept of family as a basis for trying to understand the Divine.

God discloses his attributes—his love, holiness, majesty, mercy, lovingkindness, power—but our understanding of these is (or should be) analogous; that is to say, they are not just human attributes magnified to a supersized or Godlike degree—and not simple identity. God himself is the ultimate standard of perfection for all his attributes, of which we—as his image-bearers—are but a reflection. There is no absolute contrast, either, between God's

---

8. Lakoff and Johnson, *Metaphors We Live By*, 3.
9. Lakoff and Johnson, *Metaphors We Live By*, 4.

attributes and ours. Our love—at its best—is a human reflection of divine love, not the other way around.

When God spoke to me and said that his "mighty hand" would bring about my transfer to Miami, he was referring to his divine power. "Hand" is obviously a metaphor because God does not have a literal hand, but the word "mighty" is literal. We cannot understand God's power as just human power supremely magnified. God is *the* Almighty—*and* the cause of all things. Let us not forget the words of Isaiah:

> ... for I am God, and there is no other; I am God and there is none like me, declaring the end from the beginning and from ancient times things not yet done, saying "My counsel shall stand, and I will accomplish all my purpose ... I have spoken, and I will bring it to pass; I have purposed, and I will do it." (Isa 46:9b–11 ESV)

God is also known through the names he uses of himself: King, Lord, Yahweh (his personal name), the Alpha and Omega, Lion, Lamb, Rock of our salvation.

GOD IS KNOWN THROUGH HIS ACTIONS

Finally, God is known through his actions—his mighty deeds such as creation, the exodus, the return of Israel from Babylonian exile. Supremely, however, God is known through the incarnation of Jesus Christ and the new exodus he has brought. But even here, because we have not yet seen Jesus physically, we have to rely on metaphoric language and his deeds to understand him. Jesus uses the great "I am" metaphors in John's Gospel to help reveal his identity. To know him as "the Lamb of God, who takes away the sin of the world," "the Lion of the tribe of Judah," and "the Alpha and the Omega" adds to the rich mosaic of understanding who he is.

In our finitude, it's hard to understand God through one idea. I believe it was Augustine who said that our human language is but children's toys in trying to comprehend the transcendent God. Nevertheless, God has stooped down to give us multiple names, attributes, and actions to put together a mosaic that can paint a picture of him that we can understand to help us in our prayer and praise. Even in John's exalted vision in Revelation 4, God is not visualized directly but in terms of his throne, precious jewels, smoke, etc.

I think it's obvious that there remains a certain amount of ambiguity in how we understand God because we cannot think of God apart from creaturely language, which reflects our earthly experiences. In light of the above, I am eternally grateful that God, in his divine pleasure, stooped down and spoke to me in personal, creaturely terms and changed my life with his sanctifying love. God takes delight in such things because:

> Great is the Lord, who delights in the welfare of his servant! (Ps 35:27b ESV)

GOD'S USE OF PATTERNS

Before our Miami experience I had no idea that God used patterns in history. But the authors of the Bible did. For example:

- When God announced that he would drive Israel from the land, the prophets declared that he would save Israel as he had done at the exodus—a new exodus (Isa 11:11–16). Hence, a pattern based on the exodus.
- God would raise up a new David (Hosea 3:5)—a Davidic pattern. Israel would enter into a new covenant with Yahweh (Jer 31:31)—a new covenantal pattern.
- There would be a new conquest of the land (Hosea 2:15), which would itself become a new Eden (Isa 51:3; Ezek 36:35)—an Edenic pattern.

Hamilton says this underscores a basic biblical truth worthy of italics: *"Israel's prophets used the paradigm of Israel's past to predict Israel's future."*[10]

---

10. Hamilton, *What Is Biblical Theology?*, 38

THINKING ABOUT THE EXPERIENCE

I think it's fair to say there is a unity to Scripture built on repeating patterns and themes. The disciples of Jesus may have been caught off guard, but he and his ministry were foreshadowed in the Old Testament. The disciples should have known, because the patterns were already there in the Scriptures.[11] On the road to Emmaus the resurrected Jesus had to give them a crash course "in all the Scriptures concerning himself" (Luke 24:25-27 ESV).

The Bible uses people (David, Adam), places (Eden, the wilderness), events (exodus, exile), institutions (priesthood), and structures (temple, tabernacle) as patterns or templates to build the story of Scripture. But these are not arbitrary fanciful literary devices cooked up by the authors of Scripture. The repetition of these patterns creates a grid that represents the type of thing God does or the kind of thing that happens to God's people.

SO, WHAT DO WE MAKE OF PATTERNS?

This understanding of repeating patterns is grounded in a high view of divine providence. In other words, the same God works in history and is faithful in his character. If God is at work throughout time, especially if God is faithful to his unchanging character, we would expect to discover similarities within the linear unfolding of history.

When we think this way about history, we are wandering into the general area of typology, which sees historical events as grounded within the eternal character of divine providence. History is ongoing participation in God's active providence. Boersma states that "Earlier moments in history can be types or analogues of subsequent events inasmuch as they are all grounded within the the faithful character of God's overarching providence. Thus, an analogical or typological understanding of history upstages a modern, purely linear understanding of history, and it does so

---

11. Hamilton, *What Is Biblical Theology?*, 44.

in the conviction that we can trace the faithful character of God through history."[12]

I think Hamilton would agree because he observes that when we start thinking about what typically happens, we are getting into the general area of typology. Since what has typically happened in the past, we begin to expect that this is the type of thing God will do in the future.[13] As the biblical authors noticed the type of thing God had done and interpreted these patterns in light of the promises God had made, they expected God to act in the future as he had acted in the past.[14]

WHAT ARE TYPES?

It's important that we understand at least a little about types in the Bible. In the strict sense, types are Old Testament events, persons, and institutions, among other things, that are prospective; that is, they look forward, pointing to their fulfillment. A familiar example is the Levitical priesthood in the Old Testament, which was a type that pointed ahead to fulfillment in Christ, the final high priest, who has offered the once-for-all sacrifice. Types are real accounts of what actually took place. Through installments in initial pattern (the archetype) they gather steam uphill until the type finds fulfillment in its ultimate expression (the antitype).[15] Hamilton notes, "to examine biblical typology is to examine the orchestration of the sovereign God."[16,17]

12. Boersma, *Seeing God*, 8.
13. Hamilton, *What Is Biblical Theology?*, 44.
14. Hamilton, *What Is Biblical Theology?*, 78.
15. Hamilton, *What Is Biblical Theology?*, 77.
16. Hamilton, *What Is Biblical Theology?*, 78.

17. Hamilton, *What Is Biblical Theology?*, 77–8, notes that typology must have two key features: historical correspondence and escalation. Regarding historical correspondence, for example, Noah and Moses really were preserved through waters in which others died. Escalation involves movement from the initial instance (archetype), through the installments in the pattern that reinforce the significance of the archetype. As we gather steam uphill the type finds fulfillment in its ultimate expression (the antitype). Our experience from Guadalajara to Miami was *not*, in the strict sense, an example of typology.

CONCLUSION

So why do I make a big deal about patterns, types, and language in our Christian walk? Two reasons. First, we need to pay close attention to the way God talks to us and the way we talk to him. The Bible is much more than inspired truth statements; it's full of rich metaphorical and poetic language that deserves our attention. We communicate with God using symbols and images—word pictures.

That's why I think it's mind-boggling that when God spoke to me in two visions, he used the words "my mighty hand"—obviously a metaphor for his power to accomplish what he predicted—and addressed me as "my son," coming to me as my Father in heaven. The visions and the words were not haphazard; they were not only consistent *with* the written Word of God, but they were *from* his Word and are ways he has revealed himself to his people throughout salvation history.

Scripture is a treasure trove of rich and beautiful metaphors and symbols of God and our life in Christ. We need to dwell on them and use them in our prayer and praise. I think they will be helpful on our road toward holiness and eventual glorification and perfect communion with God himself.

Second, although my prophetic and predictive visions are rare in a Western cultural setting, I do not believe that God has stopped working according to patterns in the lives of believers. Some examples may include:

- faith journeys like Abraham and Sarah based on a promise of God;
- an exodus-like experience based on the pattern of the exodus;
- an experience where we are a David facing a Goliath in our lives;
- an infertile woman, unable to conceive, praying to God and having an experience like Hannah.

The biblical patterns are there if we look for them. Contemporary experiences of God may not be as dramatic as biblical accounts, but the patterns are there for us to live within. However, we have to know our Bible well and see it as a whole—a beautiful story of redemption from creation to consummation.

When God used the words "my mighty hand," he was invoking a pattern used in Scripture: the exodus. This was not accidental but the the work of a sovereign God, the Lord of history, who can ordain and orchestrate events according to his divinely inspired patterns. Perhaps this same God is orchestrating events in your life according to his divinely inspired patterns.

3

THE EXODUS AS PATTERN

As mentioned in the previous chapter, when God said he was going to bring about my transfer to Miami by "my mighty hand," he was invoking the exodus event, the pre-eminent saving event of the Old Testament. I say this because the term "mighty hand" as used in Scripture almost always refers either directly or indirectly to the exodus and God's power to deliver his people.[1] In other

---

1. The first time the phrase "mighty hand" is used in Scripture is in the burning bush theophany in Exodus 3, in which the Lord God speaks to Moses and predicts the exodus event. In verses 19–20 God tells Moses that Pharaoh would not let the Israelites go unless compelled by a "mighty hand" (v. 19 ESV). The phrase is repeated in Exodus 6:1: "But the Lord said to Moses, 'Now you shall see what I will do to Pharaoh; for with a strong (mighty) hand he will drive them out, and with a strong (mighty) hand he will drive them out of his land'" (ESV). In Exodus 13:3 Moses exhorts the people to remember how they were brought out of Egypt by the strong (mighty) hand of the Lord. In Exodus 32:11 Moses intercedes for the people against God's wrath by remembering how he had brought them out of the land of Egypt with great power and with a "mighty hand" (ESV). The phrase, often accompanied by the term "outstretched arm," is scattered throughout the book of Deuteronomy, in which it occurs eight times, always in the context of a recital of the exodus event (4:34; 5:15; 6:21; 7:8; 7:19; 9:26; 11:2; 26:8).

God's mighty hand is also referred to in the miraculous drying of the Jordan River, allowing Israel to cross into Caanan on dry land (Josh 4:23–24). However, the template or model for that powerful act by the mighty hand of God was the drying of the Red Sea (v. 23). Daniel (9:15 ESV) also references God's "mighty hand," again in the context of the exodus. In Solomon's prayer

words, I think God chose the Old Testament exodus pattern to shape or structure my transfer to Miami.

When God spoke to me and said that his "mighty hand" would cause my transfer to Miami, he was using his own phrase for his exodus-like power to fulfill his promise. Let me put it slightly differently: God was using his vocabulary when he spoke to me. As God, he could have chosen an almost unlimited number of words, phrases, or ways to describe what he was about to do. But he didn't; he was very specific.

In addition, Elaine and I had a salvation experience. God was guaranteeing the events he was setting into motion. Second Chronicles 20:15–17 explicitly states: "Station yourselves . . . and see the salvation of the Lord on your behalf" (NASB). It's quite amazing, isn't it? Our journey was a contemporary mini-model of the broad pattern of the exodus of Israel from Egypt, when Yahweh redeemed Israel from the yoke of bondage and slavery to Pharaoh and created a people for his own possession.

You might be saying to yourself, "How was this an exodus-like experience?" After all, Elaine and I were not brought out of slavery. But the exodus did a lot of things for Israel. God's mighty hand created a people for God's own "treasured possession" in redeeming them (Deut 7:6–8 ESV). It also ultimately brought Israel into the promised land. Medical school at the University of Miami is not exactly the promised land, but it *was* promised to us by God himself and *was* like a dream come true. I cannot tell you the sheer delight we felt when God acted on our behalf and I received my acceptance letter. So, in some ways medical school was a model of sorts of the promised land for us. Also, I think it's significant that I believe God sovereignly directed us to Mexico so that he could bring us into another land of promise, which I think reflects the exodus pattern.

---

of dedication of the temple (1 Kgs 8), in a recital of Israel's history, he mentions God's "mighty hand" and "outstretched arm" (v. 42 ESV), both exodus motifs. In the same passage, Solomon directly refers to their redemption from Egyptian slavery (v. 51). Psalm 136:12, set in the context of God's enduring love, mentions how Israel was brought out of Egypt "with a strong (mighty) hand and outstretched arm" (ESV). First Peter 5:6 also refers to God's "mighty hand" but not directly in reference to the exodus.

Salvation in the Old Testament is not spiritualized. Certainly salvation refers to our justification and spiritual regeneration, but in the Old Testament salvation often means all that contributes to our flourishing and well-being.[2] When Elaine and I stationed ourselves in just the right place at just the right time as God had told us, we saw the work of a promise-keeping God working with his mighty hand on our behalf for our well-being. As such, it stands as a salvation experience. More importantly, it has created in me a profound sense that I am God's "treasured possession" (Exod 19:5 ESV). So, how could this not have been an experience based on the exodus pattern?

THINKING MORE ABOUT THE EXODUS

As I have had time over the years to think about the events of four decades ago, I have become humbled to think that the Lord of creation would use such an event as the exodus as a model for two young people in a foreign country to leave that country and go to another place—all based on a promise of God that he would bring about what he said he would.

We all know that the exodus was a huge event in salvation history, one of tremendous gravity and hard to overstate. It was Israel's founding moment and one that pervades Scripture from beginning to end. You can't read the Bible without coming across the exodus somewhere.

The death and resurrection of Jesus himself is presented in exodus and Passover terms.[3] So, for God himself to say his "mighty hand" would lead Elaine and me from one place to another was an awesome and supremely undeserved privilege.

Let's think a bit more about the exodus. Bryan Estelle states that "no other event is so basic to the fabric of both Testaments. Our concepts of deliverance . . . of God's dwelling with his people, of God taking a people for himself have their roots in this complex

---

2. Middleton, *New Heaven and a New Earth*, 79–87.
3. Estelle, *Echoes of Exodus*, 288–92.

of events."[4] He goes on the say that the exodus serves as the paradigmatic pattern for deliverance and salvation of God's people and resonates throughout virtually the entire the Bible—Psalms,[5] the prophets,[6] and the New Testament, including the Gospels and Revelation.[7]

---

4. Estelle, *Echoes of Exodus*, 4.

5. Estelle, *Echoes of Exodus*, 123–26, states that the exodus motif ripples throughout the Psalter.

For example, Psalm 114 contains allusions to the exodus event. Just as God rescued his people in the past "when he came with cosmic disturbances and intervened, so he comes in the present and future with another intervention. This pattern characterizes how God customarily treats his own people: he has acted on their behalf in the past and stands ready to act on their behalf in the future. This psalm was one in a series of psalms known as the Hallel . . . that were used regularly in celebration of the Passover and were almost certainly sung by Jesus himself at the Last Supper."

Estelle references Psalm 77 as an example of "retrojective typology." He states: "God's role in past events provides a basis for interpreting his role in present events." The psalmist hearkens back to the wonders of the exodus, but is bewildered because of God's apparent inactivity in the present.

But the tone changes in verses 11–20 toward the hope and faith of the Song of the Sea of Exodus 15. Many verbal connections and parallels exist between Exodus 15 and Psalm 77:13–20. "The psalmist reasons that just as God has worked on his people's behalf in the past, so he will deliver them in the present and the future." Although retrojective typology looks back at the wonders of God as he performed mighty deeds on behalf of his people, it has a projective aspect too. "The psalmist places himself in the midst of a journey, one grounded in the great exodus event . . . The past informs the present and the future instills hope." Estelle, *Echoes of Exodus*, 135–41.

6. Estelle says that "no prophet gives more prominence to the theme of a second exodus" than Isaiah. "Isaiah 40–55 is the linchpin in the relationship between the exodus motif and its development into the new exodus that blooms like spring in the New Testament."

The same God who acted with a mighty hand in the first exodus will act in a new way to save the exilic community from their oppressors (i.e., the Babylonians) and deliver them through the desert instead of the sea. Estelle says this portion of Scripture very clearly has the exodus in view.

Here the past becomes encouragement for future hope. By recounting his past actions and events, assurance is given to the people that their God will do new and wonderful things on their behalf. Estelle, *Echoes of Exodus*, 150–207.

7. Estelle, *Echoes of Exodus*, 1–5.

THE EXODUS AS PATTERN

Therefore, it would serve us well to understand that the exodus motif is the course of salvation in miniature. That is, it is a *synecdoche*.[8] Don't get lost here. The word "synecdoche" needs to be explained because it is important in understanding how the exodus pattern fits into salvation history. Synecdoche is a figure of speech in which a part is made to represent the whole or vice versa. For example, since I live in South Florida, I could say, "The Dolphins won by two touchdowns today." In this example the word "Dolphins" represents the entire football team. Another example would be the phrase "all hands on deck," where "hands" refers to actual people, typically sailors. So the exodus motif includes in story format the whole matrix of Christian salvation culminating in a new heaven and new earth—a new Eden and paradise.

There was only one Old Testament exodus and only one ultimate exodus inaugurated in the death and resurrection of the final Passover Lamb. But the exodus from Egypt is the template for the act of salvation by which Yahweh brings back his people from exile.

However, (and this is key to understanding our experience and many experiences of God's people), there are a number of installments in the exodus pattern. For example, David saw his deliverance from Saul as a personal exodus experience (Ps 18:15).[9] Daniel has the exodus in mind as he is confessing sin, and just before he begins asking for a new exodus he references the old with a virtual quotation of Jeremiah 32:20–21.[10] Daniel even uses the term "mighty hand" (Dan 9:15 ESV).

James Hamilton notes that there is not just one exodus. By this he means there are previews (Abraham), the exodus itself, and then a number of installments in the exodus pattern. The Mosaic (referring to Moses) exodus may therefore be looked at as a blueprint or prototype. Hamilton notes multiple instances of what he calls a "typological pattern"—repetitions of exodus-like events that give the impression that this is the kind of thing that God does

---

8. Estelle, *Echoes of Exodus*, 122.
9. Hamilton, *What Is Biblical Theology?*, 82–85.
10. Hamilton, *With the Clouds of Heaven*, 108.

for his people.[11] So, then, the experience Elaine and I had appears to be a modern-day installment of this exodus pattern—a mini-model of God's deliverance of his people by his "mighty hand."

The title of this book, *My Mighty Hand*, is not accidental. It underscores the fact that the God of creation is, indeed, almighty. We are to marvel at his deeds, not the world's. Listen to what John says in Revelation 15:3–4 (ESV), when those who had conquered the beast sang the song of Moses and of the Lamb:

> Great and amazing are your deeds, O Lord God the Almighty!
>   Just and true are your ways, O King of the nations!
>   Who will not fear, O Lord, and glorify your name?
> For you alone are holy. All nations will come and worship you,
>   for your righteous acts have been revealed.

A key purpose in sharing our testimony and writing this book is doxological: to praise the Lord of creation and marvel at his mighty deeds—at his exodus-like power to deliver, his power to bring about what he says he will. He is the one who humbles the pharaohs of the world and exalts the humble.

> Blessing and glory and wisdom and thanksgiving and honor and power and might be to our God forever and ever! Amen. (Rev 7:12b ESV)

---

11. Hamilton, *With the Clouds of Heaven*, 224.

4

"AND YOUR YOUNG MEN SHALL SEE VISIONS"

Peter in Acts 2:17, quoting Joel 2:28

THE TWO VISIONS GOD gave me four decades ago were modern-day examples of non-canonical[1] special revelation.[2] In other words, God spoke to me directly and predicted the future—in clear English sentences, but not with the authority of the Bible. The visions were given to me by the sheer grace of the sovereign God. I did not seek them, solicit them, anticipate them, or pray for them, nor did anyone lay hands on me to receive the gift of prophecy (1 Cor 12:10–11). However, I think the spiritual context is relevant

---

1. "Canon"/"canonical" refers to the preserved writings that are considered authoritative for the life and practice of the church/Christians. They are all the books of the Bible, considered to have divine authorship and be God's authoritative words in written form. The word "canon" derives from a root word meaning a measuring rod.

2. "Special revelation" is a theological term that refers to God's words addressed to specific people, such as words of the Bible and words of the Old Testament prophets, the apostles, and words of God spoken in personal address such as at Mount Sinai. This is in contradistinction to "general revelation," which refers to the existence, character, and moral law that is available to all humanity through "the law written on their hearts" (Rom 1:20; Ps 19:1–6.)

because it was a time in my life when Jesus was constantly on my mind and lips.

I can recall one evening in our apartment in Guadalajara when I had an overwhelming feeling of being at Calvary—at the foot of the cross where Jesus was crucified. Obviously, I wasn't physically there, but the feelings were so intense and the images in my mind so poignant that I felt I was there.[3] My response? I wept—because I felt unworthy before my dying Savior.

My prophetic visions occurred in a charismatic/Pentecostal setting. Elaine and I were at that time involved in a home group where spiritual gifts were taken for granted. Tongues with interpretation, prophecy, and praying for healing were regular features of worship. Jesus was exalted.

I realize that my prophetic experiences were unmerited. On the other hand, I have been aware that God had a purpose behind his mighty acts. A few years after the experience, God gave me an intense feeling and spoke in my heart that my vision experiences were so "my faith would not grow cold." This has proved true—my love for him, his Word, and his precepts has not grown cold (Ps 19:7–11; 119:11).

I have had a longstanding sense that my prophetic experiences were vouchsafed to me as a special anointing of the Holy Spirit, not to be trifled with.[4] Therefore, I have in some manner had a stewardship role to handle the experiences with the care they deserve. For example, our testimony was initially published

---

3. I don't know how to explain theologically what I experienced when I had this overwhelming sense of being at Calvary, where our Lord Jesus was crucified. In Revelation 17:3, John says he was carried away in the Spirit into the wilderness. "In the Spirit" means spiritually in a trance rather than physically. Ezekiel had similar experiences (Ezek 3:12; 8:3). I don't know whether I was in a trance or was carried in the Spirit to Calvary; I do know the experience was intense and real. My response was, I believe, appropriate to the experience.

4. Many Pentecostals and charismatics embrace baptism in the Holy Spirit *subsequent to* and *separate from* receiving the Spirit at conversion, usually manifested by speaking in tongues. This does not mean, however, that there cannot be subsequent fillings or anointings of the Spirit in which the believer is overwhelmed or even overpowered with the intense presence of of Holy Spirit.

in a small Pentecostal newspaper from Oklahoma just after it had happened. I then submitted the story to *Guideposts*, only to have it promptly rejected. Since then, Elaine and I have shared it with a few people, but have noticed wildly divergent responses. Some are deeply blessed; others don't seem to resonate with it or understand it; still others are not ready for the "spooky" or overtly supernatural aspects inherent in the experience. But I'm not responsible for the reactions of others. I am responsible to obey verses like Isaiah 12:4b:

> ... Give thanks to the Lord, call upon his name, make known his deeds among the peoples, proclaim that his name is exalted. (ESV)

However, we have been careful with whom we have shared it. We have never really made it public except for the initial foray in the small Pentecostal newspaper. But I do want to make known "his deeds among the peoples."

However, it never occurred to me four decades ago that my experience might be controversial. For years, I had no idea that my prophetic experience could be in the middle of contentious theological debates and one that some evangelicals ("cessationists") would have a hard time accepting. Some even reject such experiences on so-called theological grounds. For example, well-known evangelical and highly respected John MacArthur, in his book *Strange Fire*, states: "If the Spirit were still giving divine revelation, why wouldn't we collect and add those words to our Bibles?"[5]

I have respect for Dr. MacArthur's accomplishments and have personally benefitted from his ministry. But the theological stance of MacArthur and other cessationists does not change the fact that our experience did occur in time and space and has driven Elaine and me closer to Jesus Christ.

---

5. Quoted by Sam Storms in Brown, *Authentic Fire*, 370. See MacArthur, *Strange Fire*.

LOOKING AT IT THEOLOGICALLY

Cessationist theology, like any theological system, is built on prior theological commitments. All theological systems have built-in biases and never give us a pure reading of Scripture (which is not possible, anyway). I am not bad-mouthing theological positions or systems—I think they are necessary. I have my theological positions and biases. But I agree with Jason Meyer that although they can sharpen our understanding of the whole counsel of God, they should not first *determine* our understanding of God's Word.[6] We must be up front with our theological commitments and have self-awareness of our prior commitments and biases so we can factor these into our understanding of God's Word.[7] Dangerous, indeed, is the person who is either unaware of his biases or unwilling to admit them.

So, cessationism, like other theological positions, must reckon with experiences like ours and not simply be dismissive of the experiences of many godly believers who have supernatural experiences.[8] In fact, Jack Deere puts its very bluntly and states that one of the main reasons some cessationists deny the continuation of postbiblical revelatory gifts like prophecy and miracles is because they have never experienced them![9]

So, one would have to wonder if MacArthur were to experience the gift of prophecy, for example, whether his hard-core resistance to modern-day prophecy would soften or even vanish.

Besides, I have never entertained the thought that the visions the Spirit gave me were (or even could be) on par with the Bible. However, they have been tested by and are consistent with Scripture.

---

6. Meyer, in Wellum and Parker, eds., *Progressive Covenantalism*, 69–70.

7. Packer, in Horton, *Power Religion*, 286–99.

8. See Keener, *Miracles Today*, which documents miracles and healings in the contemporary world.

9. Deere, *Surprised by the Power of the Spirit*, 55.

BOTTOM LINE ?

I'm not going to give any theological arguments for my vision experiences because I don't think they are necessary. The important thing is that God spoke, and Elaine and I obeyed according to his sovereign promise and purpose.

5

SPIRITUAL WARFARE

> Onward, Christian Soldiers, marching as to war, with the cross of Jesus going on before.
>
> —"Onward, Christian Soldiers" (Sabine Baring-Gould, 1865)

OUR EXPERIENCE FOUR DECADES ago was a spiritual battle. God fought for us against Satan and the powers of evil. Recall Bill Cooper's prophetic words for us not to believe "this evil report" and to "pursue the enemy." Who can forget the wonderful verses that God gave us in the heat of the battle: "Humble yourselves, therefore, under the mighty hand of God, that he may exalt you at the proper time . . . your adversary, the devil, prowls about like a roaring lion seeking someone to devour. But resist him, firm in your faith" (1 Pet 5:6–9 TEV).

To top it off, 2 Chronicles 20:15–17, given to us that eventful Labor Day weekend, says, ". . . thus says the Lord to you. 'Do not fear or be dismayed . . . for the battle is not yours but God's. Tomorrow go down against them . . . You need not fight in this battle; station yourselves, stand and see the salvation of the Lord on your behalf . . . Do not fear or be dismayed; tomorrow go out to face them, for the Lord is with you'" (NASB). All the "evil reports"

SPIRITUAL WARFARE

or lies that Satan used to try to stop us clearly demonstrate that this was a battle being waged by more than "flesh and blood."

SPIRITUAL WARFARE AND THE BELIEVER

I'm sure all of us have had times in our Christian walk when we have sensed that we are in a spiritual battle of some kind. Even though the term "spiritual warfare" is not mentioned in Scripture, it's a meaningful phrase because the Bible contains lots of battle imagery. Our go-to verse is Ephesians 6:12, which says, "For we do not wrestle against flesh and blood, but against the rulers, against the authorities, against the cosmic powers over this present darkness, against the spiritual forces of evil in the heavenly places" (ESV).

The big question is: What does Paul mean by "powers" and "spiritual forces"? Christians have wrestled with the meaning of these and come up with various answers and, hence, different views of spiritual warfare. In plain terms, Bible-believing Christians disagree about what spiritual warfare is.

Are we surprised, therefore, that there are many Christian books on spiritual warfare from almost every point of view—all trying to help us get a handle on things . . . on how to understand our battle with evil and how to respond?[1] One of my favorites is edited by Beilby and Eddy[2] and cogently presents four basic

---

1. There are many fine books available on spiritual warfare. Included would be: White, *Believer's Guide to Spiritual Warfare*; Cook and Lawless, *Spiritual Warfare in the Storyline of Scripture*; Kraft, *Christianity with Power*; Arnold, *3 Crucial Questions about Spiritual Warfare*. Of course, the classic book on the subject is C. S. Lewis's *The Screwtape Letters*.

2. The reader is referred to Beilby and Rhodes, *Understanding Spiritual Warfare*. Certainly the models discussed in this book do not exhaust the possible ways of looking at spiritual warfare, but I think they represent the four most common ones. While there still appears to be a general consensus in the modern Western evangelical world regarding the existence and nature of spiritual beings, including Satan and demons, perspectives vary on questions such as how much authority and influence these powers of darkness exert in today's world. I doubt many American evangelicals would question the New Testament record on exorcisms and cosmic warfare, but would hesitate about

models. Of course, models of spiritual warfare are not presented as such in Scripture—models are things that we build to help us understand something. However, in my efforts to make sense of what happened four decades ago, I have looked at different models to try to figure out what exactly happened in terms of our spiritual battle.

MODELS OF SPIRITUAL WARFARE

Two Irrelevant Models

Two models of spiritual warfare discussed in Beilby and Eddy have no obvious relevance to our experience. The first, strategic-level spiritual warfare (SLSW), wages spiritual warfare against what are called "territorial spirits"—high-ranking demons or evil spirits who are assigned to geopolitical territories and social networks such as cities and countries and hold them in spiritual captivity so they cannot respond to the light of the gospel. These high-ranking evil spirits keep large numbers of humans in spiritual bondage with resulting rampant injustice, oppression, hunger, disease, racism, human trafficking, greed, and violence. I think you can see why this model doesn't relate to our experience four decades ago.

A second model is the so-called world-systems model, made famous by Walter Wink in his *Powers* trilogy,[3] and which gives no ontological status to Satan. In other words, Wink does not believe in a personal devil, a belief he calls a piece of "medieval superstition." Wink understands Satan as a symbol for the evil that permeates society and the structures of society, such as institutions (rapacious multinational corporations, ideologies, oppressive governments, etc.) that oppress and dominate. Therefore, when world

---

such matters on the contemporary scene. In other words, if a local Baptist or Presbyterian church were to have an exorcism, it would cause quite a stir, if not a split. Therefore, there is much diversity of perspective regarding the nature and practice of spiritual warfare.

3. See: Wink, *Naming the Powers; Unmasking the Powers; Engaging the Powers*.

structures become oppressive, demonic systems of domination, it becomes the responsibility of the church to name, unmask, and engage them. We can scratch this model off.

Third Model Hits Home

So, on we go to the third model of spiritual warfare, the so-called ground-level deliverance model, championed by Gregory Boyd and clearly stated in his book *God at War: The Bible and Spiritual Conflict*,[4] and discussed in Beilby and Eddy. This model recognizes, among other things, the importance of dealing directly with personal demonic agents. Boyd zeroes in on cosmic conflict in the ministry of Jesus. His approach to Jesus' entire ministry is one of warfare and head-on confrontation with the "prince of this world," Satan.

Jesus' teachings, exorcisms, healings, and atoning work on the cross were acts of war, pushing back the kingdom of darkness and advancing the kingdom of God—God's rule or reign. So, Boyd sees an "apocalyptic" Jesus, advancing the kingdom against the frontiers of darkness, and views the cosmos a war zone of good versus evil. The disciples, therefore, understood that their central mission was to oppose such evil and overthrow it.[5]

I think it's easy to agree that cosmic conflict is prominent in Scripture. First of all, Jesus believed that Satan was the ruler of this world (John 12:31). However, he had come to "cast him out." The very first Christian sermon, according to Luke, centered on Christ's cosmic victory (Acts 2:32–6). When Jesus sent out his disciples to preach and heal, they were excited that the demons had submitted to them in his name. Jesus' response? He had seen "Satan fall like lightning from heaven" (Luke 10:18b ESV).

The theme of victory over cosmic foes pervades the entire New Testament. It's not exactly top secret that Psalm 110 is the most frequently cited passage in the New Testament:

---

4. Boyd, *God at War*.
5. Boyd, *God at* War, 235.

The Lord says to my Lord: "Sit at my right hand, until I make my your enemies your footstool." (Ps 110:1 ESV)

THE BIG DISCONNECT

But we don't live in New Testament times, you might say. For example, here in South Florida, one of our megachurches has a sticker that goes on the back of vehicles of its members. It is a cross (†), then an equal sign (=), then a heart (♥), all symbolizing the fact that Jesus died on the cross because he loves us—true as far as it goes. However, a sticker with a †, =, and sword (⟍) or other symbol of war would not be understood by most Americans because it does not fit our sensibilities—Jesus is a loving Savior, not a combatant. God is love.

But that's the point—he *is* a combatant. What the New Testament affirms is that at the cross Jesus disarmed and triumphed over the devil and all the "principalities and powers." First-century hearers of the gospel would have had no difficulty in accepting this, nor would contemporary developing-world believers. So, there seems to be a huge disconnect between our North American naturalistic worldview—colored by the Enlightenment—and the New Testament.

WHAT IS APOCALYPTIC?

I mentioned a few paragraphs earlier that Boyd saw an "apocalyptic" Jesus, advancing the kingdom of God against the kingdom of darkness. I would bet that few of us understand what the word "apocalyptic" means in the biblical sense. So we need to take a time-out. The apocalyptic framework is really important in understanding the gospel because it permeated the New Testament worldview and the mind of Jesus.

The word "apocalyptic" floats around in our popular culture but rarely in its biblical form. For most, it means an extreme event—especially one accompanied by real or imagined signs of the end of the world. No doubt some will default to a bizarre fixation on a science-fiction-like "zombie apocalypse" or other catastrophic collapse of civilization. So, I think the church needs to take back the real meaning of the word for her own self-understanding.[6]

"Apocalyptic" in the biblical sense is a worldview in which the war of the ages is being waged between God and the enemy, who deploys the principalities and powers. This battle on the heavenly front is played out on earth in human affairs—battles waged not with worldly weapons but with the spiritual armor of God (Eph 6:11–17). An apocalyptic worldview is a way of viewing history, which is the arena of God's activity. It colors *the way we see historical events*. Human affairs take on a different meaning when seen from the perspective of biblical apocalyptic theology. So, when Boyd sees an apocalyptic Jesus advancing the kingdom of God against the frontiers of darkness and views the cosmos as a war zone of good versus evil, he is on solid ground. [7]

Fleming Rutledge, in her book *The Crucifixion: Understanding the Death of Jesus Christ*, makes a nice point that Jesus' massive struggle in the garden of Gethsemane the night he was betrayed and arrested is often misperceived.[8] She believes Jesus' extreme physical distress ("his sweat became like great drops of blood," Luke 22:44 ESV) while he was struggling in prayer to the Father, asking his cup of suffering be taken away from him, was a massive struggle with diabolical opposition. We all know this story but do

---

6. The word "apocalyptic" in the biblical sense encompasses a worldview in which the truly significant battle is the ongoing one between God and the enemy, who deploys the principalities and powers (Eph 2:2). This contest on a heavenly level is played out on the earthly level by struggles large and small in human affairs—battles fought not with worldly weapons but with the spiritual armor of God (Eph 6:11–17).

Fleming Rutledge believes that in our secular culture the biblical meaning of the word is lost—all the more reason for the church to reclaim it for her own self-understanding. Apocalyptic is not some bizarre fixation on imagined catastrophic events (zombie apocalypse) but a comprehensive worldview and a way of seeing historical events. It was so pervasive in Jesus' time that it is reasonable to assume that he shared it. The reader is referred to Rutledge, *Crucifixion*, ch. 9, for a good discussion of apocalyptic.

7. Boyd, *God at War*, 235.

8. Rutledge, *Crucifixion*, 371–75.

we really know that in this garden, on the eve of the crucifixion, God was initiating the definitive confrontation with the ruler of this world? Do we know that the judgment on the prince of this world—and, therefore, of the cosmos itself—coincides with the judgment that Jesus takes upon himself, in our place? What Jesus was doing is invading enemy territory—taking back for himself the world he created.

BE WATCHFUL

As Jesus was on the battlefield, so are we. This may sound strange to many of us evangelicals. But we are to be disciplined ("be sober") and vigilant ("be watchful"), because the enemy is untiring. We cannot be on a spiritual vacation or cruise because the predatory activity of the devil ("like a lion seeking someone to devour") is real (1 Pet 5:8 NIV). It is part of the New Testament thought world ... part of the gospel. The gospel of Christ means deliverance from the tyranny of outside forces into a realm of light and life.

Neither in 1 Peter nor in today's preaching is apocalyptic thinking disposable; it's part of the good news. The gospel is a message of deliverance from the grip of evil and death ... from the kingdom of darkness into the glorious kingdom of Jesus Christ. Satan still tries to stop us, but "we are more than conquerors" (Rom 8:37 ESV) in Christ. This is bedrock and part and parcel of being a believer. We are in a cosmic conflict with a cosmic enemy.

BEST EXPLANATORY MODEL

In sum, I think Boyd's model comes closest to what Elaine and I experienced on our spiritual journey. We came into direct confrontation with the powers of evil incarnated in persons who tried (perhaps unwittingly) to snuff out God's purposes and promises. Satan used persons in the administrative structure at the School of Medicine to discourage us and try to get us to give up—a cosmic battle being played out in human affairs. In addition, what about that wild-looking female along the Florida Turnpike who told us to turn back because Hurricane David had destroyed Miami? Do you really think she was an agent of light? The "evil reports" such as my denial letter were designed by Satan to discourage us to give up. All these schemes by Satan, who was working through human agency, were deceits. But pursuing the enemy and believing the good reports (the Word of God and his prophetic word) was the right strategy to defeat Satan and his deception. In the end, Boyd's model of cosmic conflict seems to fit our experience the best because God was indeed invading Satan's territory and pushing back the frontiers of darkness.

FOURTH MODEL RELEVANT

However, I believe these models are fluid and perhaps even overlapping to some degree. Believers can have their feet in more than one.

I like a quote of Dean Sherman from his book *Spiritual Warfare for Every Christian*:

> Some think spiritual warfare is only deliverance. Others emphasize pulling down strongholds in the heavenliness. Still others say spiritual warfare is doing the works of Jesus—preaching, teaching, and living the truth. Yet another group claims all this is impractical. They claim we should focus on feeding the hungry, resisting racism, and speaking out against social injustice. I believe we have to do it all. Pulling down strongholds is only important if people are led to Christ as a result. However, some are deaf to the preaching of the Gospel until we deal with hindering powers. And some can't break through into victory until bondage is broken in their lives. We must do it all as appropriate, and as God leads.[9]

I would agree with Sherman for the most part because he seems to be trying to keep a sense of balance of the various models we have discussed. However, Sherman is an advocate of SLSW,

9. Sherman, *Spiritual Warfare for Every Christian*, 187.

so I would not agree with him on "pulling down strongholds in the heavenlies" if he means direct confrontation with territorial spirits. However, he is absolutely correct that we do need God's guidance in spiritual warfare.

Nevertheless, I have found that through this life-changing experience I have developed a deep appreciation for a fourth model, the "classical model," ably articulated by the late theologian and counselor David Powlison in *Power Encounters: Reclaiming Spiritual Warfare*.[10] Powlison's book focuses on the weapons of the Word of God, repentance, faith, and obedience. His model is what many of us would call "discipleship" or "sanctification"—the lifelong and sometimes painful journey of becoming more Christlike.

None of us is immune from the temptations and sin that arise so easily from our fleshly sinful nature. Fighting the world-flesh-devil is the lifelong moral struggle that all of us believers face—the old-man/new-man struggle that the apostle Paul labors to talk about in Romans 7. In plain terms, in the classical model, spiritual warfare is basically synonymous with Christian growth and discipleship—a model that many evangelicals would feel comfortable with.

Since my prophetic experience, I have struggled like every believer with the triad of flesh-world-devil. Sometimes the struggles have been painful. The travails of career, family, finances, modern-day stress, lust for the things of this world—all have weighed on me subsequent to my prophetic visions. But (and this is big) I have never forgotten what God did for Elaine and me. God's mighty deeds are etched in my soul. Listen to these verses from Deuteronomy:

> You shall fear the Lord your God. You shall serve him and hold fast to him . . . He is your praise. He is your God, who has done for you these great and terrifying things that your eyes have seen. (Deut 10:20–21 ESV)

My old-man/new-man struggles have been set within the context of our holy experience of over four decades ago. I would

---

10. Powlison, *Power Encounters*.

hope the experience has made me more like Christ, "in whom are hidden all the treasures of wisdom and knowledge" (Col 2:3 ESV).

I believe that my experience four decades ago has had a positive effect on my sanctification and spiritual growth and that a strong biblical argument can be made that witnessing God's mighty acts should foster our growth as believers. I like the book of Deuteronomy because it is a rich treasure trove of spiritual nuggets that can instruct us. For example, Deuteronomy 11:1–12, which is addressed to the Moab generation of Israelites about to cross over into the promised land, demonstrates the importance of being an eyewitness to God's "majesty, his mighty hand" (v. 2b NIV), and the subsequent requirement to obedience. God tells that generation, "But it was your own eyes that saw all these great things the Lord has done. Observe therefore all the commands I am giving you today, so that you may have the strength to go in and take over the land that you are crossing the Jordan to possess . . ." (Deut 11:7–8 NIV).

May God give me and all of us the strength to cross the finish line so that we may inherit the ultimate promised land.

6

THE KINGDOM OF GOD IN MIAMI

I VIEW OUR GUADALAJARA-TO-MIAMI journey of four decades ago, in no small part, in terms of the kingdom of God, which may be surprising. Even more surprising, however, is that when our actual experience happened, I don't recall ever having heard of the kingdom, let alone what it was or signified.

My interest in God's kingdom began in 1989 when I was enrolled in the Masters of Missiology program at Fuller Theological Seminary via correspondence and wrote a paper for a course in the Theology of Mission under Dr. Arthur F. Glasser. At that time my wife and I were medical missionaries in the then-named Zaïre (now the Democratic Republic of the Congo), so the paper I wrote was quite naturally about medical missions. However, the course required the paper to be written under the rubric of the kingdom of God, about which I had known absolutely nothing.

My required reading introduced me to such scholars as John Bright and George Eldon Ladd, whose books[1,2] pointed me to the fact that that the kingdom of God (or kingdom of heaven) was the central theme of Jesus during his earthly ministry. So, I searched Scripture and discovered that Jesus proclaimed the kingdom in his

1. Ladd, *The Gospel of the Kingdom*.
2. Bright, *The Kingdom of God*.

parables (especially in Matthew 13), in the Sermon on the Mount and is a recurring theme in his instructions to his disciples.

As a missionary ministering in a cross-cultural setting, I also became familiar with the perspectives of African theologians regarding the kingdom, especially regarding healing. I also became acquainted with the excellent work of missionary anthropologists like Charles Kraft and Paul Hiebert.

As a result of my study of God's kingdom, it is my belief that what Elaine and I experienced was an in-breaking of the kingdom of God and a foretaste of the "powers of the age to come" (Heb 6:5 NRSV). Before I go any further, however, I need to say that even though the kingdom of God was a central theme of Jesus, it's my experience that most believers don't understand it. (Don't worry! The kingdom is not an easy concept to grasp. I'll try my best to explain it.)

WHAT IS THE KINGDOM?

I have also noticed that the kingdom is not preached much or taught in most evangelical churches. Most of the time when I have heard the kingdom of God mentioned by clergy and laity alike it's in the context of "building God's kingdom." This, however, seems to betray a faulty theology and a fundamental misunderstanding of the kingdom because the kingdom of God is not primarily a place, location or a realm.[3]

Anthony Hoekema states:

> "The kingdom of God ... is to be understood as the reign of God dynamically active in human history through Jesus Christ, the purpose of which is redemption of God's people from sin and from demonic powers, and the final establishment of the new heavens and the new earth ... The kingdom must not be understood as merely salvation of certain individuals of even as the reign of God in

---

3. Hoekema, *The Bible and the Future*, 44–45.

the hearts of his people; it means nothing less than the reign of God over his entire created universe."[4]

Most scholars agree the kingdom is the *fact* (italics added) of God's rule or reign—or his saving sovereignty. Ladd states that once this is realized, "we can go through the New Testament and find passage after passage where this meaning is evident, where the Kingdom is not a realm or a people but God's reign."[5]

Moreover, the kingdom of God is virtually a synonym for the gospel rightly understood. The message Jesus preached was the "good news of the kingdom" (Mt 4:23 NRSV). This term recurs in Matthew 9:35 and 24:14 and becomes "this gospel" in 26:13 (NRSV). Even Luke, when summarizing the content of Paul's preaching to the Gentiles used the utterly non-Hellenistic phrase "the kingdom of God" (Acts 28:31 NRSV).

Jesus himself associated eternal life with the kingdom of God. In Matthew 19:23-25—the passage concerning the rich young ruler, who asked what he needed to do to have eternal life—Jesus' answer in this context seems to equate the kingdom of God/heaven with eternal life and being saved. In fact, according to the Synoptics, to be saved is to enter the kingdom of God and to inherit eternal life (Mt 19:16-25; Mk 10:17-26; Lk 18:18-26).

WHEN WILL THE KINGDOM COME?

To make things more interesting (or more complicated for those of us who like things simple), it seems like a majority of scholars have reached a consensus that the kingdom is in some sense both present and future. Some of the most characteristic gospel sayings are those which speak of a present coming of the kingdom. According to Mark 1:15, the kingdom has already come, and the time of fulfillment is already here. Luke 17:20–21 is crystal clear: the kingdom of God had arrived. Jesus unambiguously affirms in

---

4. Hoekema, *The Bible and the Future*, 45.

5. Ladd, *The Gospel of the Kingdom*, 21. Ladd is a well-known and highly respected scholar on kingdom and on eschatology in general.

Matthew 12:28 that the kingdom "has come" and makes it clear that it is the exercise of God's saving sovereignty that has dawned. In addition, the casting out of demons is a sign of the presence of the kingdom (Mt 12:28).

But the kingdom is also future. Passages like the Olivet Discourse, statements of the apostle Paul in 1 Thessalonians 4-5 and 2 Thessalonians 1 are clearly about a future coming of the Son of Man—a final coming of Christ in glory to set up his Messianic kingdom. John's Revelation also has a similar pattern, climaxed in Rev 11:15: "The kingdom of the world has become the kingdom of our Lord and of his Christ, and he shall reign forever and ever." (NRSV)

TENSIONS IN THE KINGDOM

Derek Morphew, in his outstanding book on the kingdom,[6] states that the New Testament understanding of the kingdom can be summarized in four statements:

- The kingdom will come
- The kingdom has come
- The kingdom is coming immediately
- The kingdom will be delayed

He believes this is precisely where part of the mystery lies and that these truths must be held in creative tension with each other.

The kingdom of God and the above statements of it being present, yet future, almost here, yet delayed may be hard for us to understand if we fail to grasp the biblical concept of time. That is, we need to see things more from God's point of view (although that's fully impossible because he is an eternal being and we are

---

6. Morphew, *Breakthrough*. This is probably the best book I have read on the kingdom go God in terms of edifying the believer. Outstanding. The 1991 edition is the best edition in my opinion.

finite creatures). But, according to the New Testament we, as redeemed believers, live in two ages.[7,8,9]

The present age is evil (Gal 1:4) and ruled by Satan (Jn 12:31), the prince of this world. This age is characterized by sin, disease, corruption, hostility to the gospel and death. All people, believers and unbelievers, live in this age, which will not terminate until the second coming of Christ, at which time God will judge all mankind and usher believers into their full enjoyment of the kingdom blessings—a new heaven and new earth.

However, the New Testament also speaks of the age to come (eternal life, cf. Mk 10:30) or the future age. This age is characterized by righteousness, immortality, the resurrected life, glory and all the things that come to mind when we think of eternal life. However, (and this is where things can get somewhat perplexing) the age to come or future age is not strictly future but has penetrated this present evil age. F.F. Bruce states it well:

> "At Christ's first coming the age to come invaded this present age; at his coming in glory the age to come will have altogether superseded this present age. Between the comings the two ages overlap; the people of Christ live temporally in this present age while spiritually they

---

7. The New Testament has much to say about the ages: Mt 12:32; Lk 16:8; Mk 10:30; Eph 2:7; Heb 6:5; 1 Tim 6:17.

8. Waldron, *The End Times Made Simple*, 42.

9. I think one of the problems in understanding the fact that the kingdom of God is both present and future, imminent and delayed is that we, as creatures, live in time. That is to say, we sense events in succession, one after another. To say that we live "between the times" when two ages coexist poses problems for us as time-bound creatures. God, on the other hand, as eternal Creator is timeless (Ps 90:2). He sees all time equally (Ps 90:4; 2 Pet 3:8), and his relationship to time is qualitatively different than ours. He is timeless and does not experience a succession of events like we do. God somehow stands above time and is able to see it all as present in his consciousness—that is, God sees all of history equally present. Yet it is evident from Scripture and from experience that God acts within time. As Lord of time, he can predict the future, bring it about rule over it and use it for his own purposes. See Grudem, chapter 11 of *Systematic Theology* for a good discussion from which the above was taken.

belong to the heavenly kingdom and enjoy by anticipation the life of the age to come."[10]

This creates a tension because the present evil age ruled by Satan goes on, yet the kingdom of God, which is future, has come in the present, with its power and blessings. This creates an overlap of the ages or interim period during the church age. Two ages coexist. Most believers, I would say, contrast our lives in the present with our lives in the future by use of the words "earth" and "heaven." In other words, our present existence is on earth but our future existence after we die will be with the Lord in a place called heaven. This is what is taught and preached in most evangelical pulpits today. Many of our hymns reflect this perspective.

I would also be willing to say that few of us believers understand or even know that we are living in two ages, where one age (the age to come) has penetrated the other (the present age) so that there is an overlap. Satan has already been defeated at the cross by Jesus' atoning work, yet the present evil age goes on—for now. So, the time between the resurrection of Christ and his second coming is a time of the overlapping of two ages, one evil and one righteous, so that we, the church, live "between the times."

ALREADY BUT NOT YET

Therefore, we live in an "already but not yet" situation because the kingdom is already here in its fulfillment (Mk 1:15) but not yet in its consummation or its finality (Rev 11:15). Morphew states, "Everything that is still to happen at the Second Coming has already happened in Jesus Christ. It has not taken place in complete finality, but in a real, anticipatory sense."[11]

Morphew goes on to say that the Old Testament prophets often held together events of the immediate and the distant future in one prediction. This is a prophetic view of history, with more than one fulfillment in multiple events. The kingdom can be

---

10. Bruce, *Commentary on the Book of Acts*, 35.
11. Morphew, *Breakthrough*, 66.

both immediate and distant without any sense of contradiction. I'm going to quote Morphew because I believe this is important in understanding the kingdom:

> "We must hold on to each strand of Jesus' teaching. The kingdom of God is future, immediate, present and delayed. Only when we hold these 'contradictory' strands together can we really understand the glory and power of the kingdom of God in Jesus Christ. Perhaps it is only the prophetic vision that can begin to see things through the eyes of God with whom a thousand years are one day. Armed with this prophetic view of history, we can come to terms with the mysterious nature of the kingdom: *It breaks through from the future into the present in successive interventions of God.*"[12]

Morphew continues by noting that that which is of the future and its power are already present in an unexpected way. So we can say that the future is already present, but its presence is not exhaustive.[13]

The present enjoyment of a future reality reflects the basic eschatological framework of the New Testament, in which this age and the age to come have so overlapped that we believers living still in the present evil age may enter into actual enjoyment of the powers and blessings of the age to come.[14] The blessings of the future no longer remain in the future in a place called "heaven" but have become to some degree present experience in this age. Hebrews 6:5 witnesses to those who have "tasted the powers of the age to come ..." When Paul speaks about the first fruits of the Spirit in Romans 8:22–23, he is referring not to mere promise, but to real experience.

Jon Rutven so aptly states that "wherever the Spirit displaces the kingdom of darkness in its various manifestations of evil, whether sin, sickness or demonic possession, the Kingdom of God has provisionally arrived. Such victories of repentance, healing or

---

12. Morphew, *Breakthrough*, 65.
13. Morphew, *Breakthrough*, 66.
14. Ladd. *A Theology of the New Testament*, 305.

other restoration from the demonic world represent a continuing, though partial experience of the fully realized and uncontested reign of God to come."[15]

I agree with Morphew's assessment of the kingdom and its implications for Christian living. We live in two ages until the end of this age, when the kingdom will be consummated and fully revealed and, at which time, we will see God in his fullness and in which there will be no more sin, pain, or suffering. This was the hope of the prophets, and it is our hope. Until then, we live "between the times."

LIVING AS KINGDOM CITIZENS

The powers of the coming age have been present since Jesus came. To grasp this is to re-orientate our perspective. Every Christian should live as kingdom citizens—constantly expecting the in-breaking of the kingdom but knowing that it is also delayed. When we experience the powers of the kingdom we partake in the down-payment of our future redemption. When the kingdom draws near, we have a foretaste, knowing that our final future will be infinitely more of the same.[16]

I love Morphew's description of kingdom living. He says that understanding the kingdom ...makes us patient with what fails to happen. It is always here almost here, delayed, and future. Every promise of God every prophetic word every calling every ministry we engage in, has the mysterious sense of continually delayed by God yet just around the corner. We live tasting, yet with our mouths watering; filled and yet hungry; satisfied and yet longing; having all, yet needing all.[17]

He goes on: the very nature of the Christian life finds its meaning within this context. We are here, almost here, delayed, future people. We are saved, being saved, and will be saved. We live

---

15. Rutven, *On the Cessation of the Charismata*, 175.
16. Morphew, *Breakthrough*, 83.
17. Morphew, *Breakthrough*, 84.

between the times. We are already-not-yet people. Two ages coexist within us and we live simultaneously in two ages. The world around us lives in one age, one dimension ... we have eternal life, the life of the future age. We live in this eschatological tension and cannot escape it. It's the air we currently breathe.[18]

I cannot help but agree with the profound insights that Morphew offers us regarding the kingdom of God and its implication for the lives of believers. I think many of us have had the kingdom draw near at some point in our lives—when we have experienced the "powers of the age to come (Heb 6:5)." This is certainly what Elaine and I experienced four decades ago, when God's kingdom broke through into our lives and displaced the rule of Satan. Nothing was going to stop what God had predicted and promised—no evil reports, no intimidating secretaries trying to get us to give up our hopes and efforts, no broken-down vehicle, no hurricane, no wild-looking female trying to get us to turn back. Nothing—because the kingdom of God inaugurated by Jesus does not consist in talk, but in δύναυις (miracle power) (1 Cor 4:20).

---

18. Morphew, *Breakthrough*, 87.

7

WHOM DO YOU TRUST?

> Trust and obey, for there's no other way . . .
> —1887 hymn by John Sammis

PART 1: LESSONS FROM ABRAHAM

WHO COULD HAVE ORCHESTRATED the chain of events leading to my transfer to Miami? Certainly not myself—nor Elaine. I'm not an oddsmaker or very good at figuring out probability, but the chances of Elaine and I being in the admissions office of a major medical school ("ready to begin classes" and "claiming my position") the same day a student happened to take a leave of absence, after I had been rejected for transfer and having traveled over two thousand miles a few months earlier after having dropped out of another medical school, were . . . let's say, infinitesimal. Zilch.

Most of our family and friends were courteous skeptics, most likely because they had a gut feeling that we could not possibly succeed. It made zero sense. Some thought we were crazy for going out on a limb like we did. (But we were crazy only until I was accepted. Then the tables were turned and then *they* looked a little crazy for having not believed us.) Everyone was asking the same question: "How did we *know* these things were going to happen?" The answer? Because God had spoken.

Like Abram and Sarai

Mere human effort could not have made events like this happen apart from God's promise. Again, our experience appears to follow a pattern seen in Scripture. For example, Elaine and I, like Abram and Sarai, left one country for another, trusting God would be faithful to his promise. I think it's highly significant that the events—both in our case and in Abram and Sarai's—were initiated by a promise of God.

So, in order to unpack our experience a bit, I have found the Genesis text describing God's promises to Abram and his response to be pure gold. As we look at the text we note that verse 12:4a is key: "So Abram went, as the Lord had told him . . ." (ESV). Abram simply obeyed in response to God's promises in verses 2–3. The Genesis text doesn't record Abram sending letters or prayer chains to family and friends on papyrus asking for prayer.

The narrative states that God commanded Abram to leave his country and go to a land God would show him. Neither did Elaine and I bother sending prayer chains and letters to friends and family. We simply obeyed the promise of God ("You will transfer to Miami this summer by my mighty hand."), knowing he would be faithful. Elaine and I, like Abram and Sarai, left one country for another, trusting God would be faithful to his promise.

Conditional or Unconditional?

One hot-button issue among scholars is whether God's covenant with Abraham was conditional or unconditional. In other words, would God have kept his promise apart from anything Abraham did or didn't do? Certainly, if we look at Genesis 15, it appears that the covenant was all on God—unconditional. God actually put a potential curse on himself if he didn't keep his end of the bargain.

In other words, God obligated himself to Abraham if he would not keep his covenant and fail to fulfill his promise.

But wait! Things aren't so simple. Gentry and Wellum, in their magisterial *Kingdom Through Covenant,* note that God made commitments and promises to Abraham but needed his obedience within a covenant relationship in order for the promise to be fulfilled. So, the unconditional emphasis of Genesis 15 does not obviate the need for Abraham's obedience. In other words, the fulfillment of God's promises is "clearly linked to the obedience of Abraham."[1]

Oren Martin agrees. Both unconditional and conditional elements exist in the covenant God made with Abram. The Abrahamic covenant was conditional. The "So Abram went" of Genesis 12:4 fulfills the divine command to "Go from your country" of 12:1. That is, Abram's response was necessary. But as demonstrated in the covenant ceremony in Genesis 15, Abram can do nothing to enter into the promise. He can only rely on the Lord to fulfill his word.[2] The covenant was unconditional.

Here's the bottom line: *ultimately,* the grace of God—not the obedience of Abraham—is foundational. Fulfillment of the promise does not depend on Abram's ability, but on God's, who is powerfully able to do what he has promised. Gentry and Wellum, quoting Grueneberg, note that "human obedience does not enable something other than can come from God's promise."[3]

Even though Abraham's obedience was a necessary part, it was not the basis for God's gracious blessings. In other words, God did not bless Abraham *because he obeyed.* Abraham's obedience was *instrumental* to the fulfillment of God's promise. The *means of fulfillment* was through Abraham's obedience.[4] God used Abraham's obedience to bring about his promise because the ultimate fulfillment of the covenant was grounded in his promises.

---

1. Gentry and Wellum, *Kingdom Thought Covenant*, 323.

2. Martin, *Bound for the Promised Land*, 63–69.

3. Gentry and Wellum, *Kingdom Through Covenant*, 323, quoting Grueneberg, *Abraham, Blessing and the Nations*, 223, 224, 226.

4. Martin, *Bound for the Promised Land*, 70.

In a nutshell, Abraham has served as a biblical and spiritual template for me to understand our experience, when Elaine and I responded in faith to God's promise and left one country for another to inherit the promise of God. In the end, our journey was the gracious and unmerited work of the sovereign God. The ultimate fulfillment was not grounded in our obedience but in God's faithfulness to his promise.

Misreading God's Promises

I'm probably going into more detail than most readers would like about Abraham's experience. However, the nuts and bolts of how obedience, trust, and God's promises all fit together are really important to understand for practical reasons. Many of our friends and even family misread how God worked in our faith journey from Guadalajara to Miami. For example, I can't tell you how many told Elaine and me that God rewarded our mountain-moving faith by getting me into medical school at Miami. There seemed to be a "wow" impression that since we took such dramatic, bridge-burning risks (some would call them "stupid"), God kept his end of the bargain. This reveals a sort of cause-and-effect relationship in peoples' minds. I think there was (and still is) some confusion about how faith/trust and obedience factor in to God's promises.

Here's how I see it. I was going to transfer to Miami because God had ordained it. It was going to happen. God came to me in the form of visions and made a promise of something that he had already foreordained to occur. But God needed our obedience instrumentally because he always needs us (humans) to accomplish his purposes in time and space—in history. You may see this like a puppeteer pulling the strings of his puppets, but Elaine and I had wills and made decisions and took real risks. (Such is the mystery of divine sovereignty and human responsibility.) At the end of the day, our actions alone would not and could not have made events like this happen apart from God's ordained sovereign promises and purpose.

Cannot Force God

We cannot bully, sweet-talk, force, or coax God to make events like this happen. This is magical thinking. It must be according to God's sovereign will. After I had transferred to Miami, there was another married medical student at Guadalajara who was so impressed by our testimony that he felt that God was leading him in the same direction. So, he applied to the School of Medicine at Miami, sent out prayer letters to friends and members of his church, had people praying for God to work, and waited. Elaine and I met with him and his wife in Miami, and they were upbeat—confident that God would honor their desires. But it never happened. He was turned downed for transfer—a very bitter and disillusioning disappointment.

I again quote Grueneberg, whose insights are profound regarding the obedience of Abraham: "Abraham's obedience is not blind, a matter of outward performance or of submission to arbitrary divine whims. It rather stems from his relationship with a God who . . . remains faithful to his promises (vv. 16–18), who is working for good even when demanding something painful or puzzling . . ."[5]

Well . . . Elaine and I obeyed and certainly did some puzzling things in the eyes of many, but we inherited the promises of God—because the blessings of God are for those who "trust and obey" within a relationship with the sovereign God of the universe. We inherited the promise of God by walking in faith and, like Abraham, our faith was perfected as we obeyed (Jas 2:22).

PART 2: LESSONS FROM ISAIAH

Trusting in God is a big deal to me. So, we are going straight to the book of Isaiah to get us up to snuff on trusting God. John Oswalt, in his wonderful commentary on Isaiah,[6] comments that in

---

5. Gentry and Wellum, *Kingdom Through Covenant*, 323, quoting Grueneberg, *Abraham, Blessing and the Nations*, 223, 224, 226.

6. Oswalt, *Book of Isaiah*.

chapters 7–39 a major theme is trusting in Yahweh. Serving God necessarily involves trusting him—you must take risks for him. So, we are going to look at two Judean kings, both of whom faced overwhelming odds but were asked to trust Yahweh. One passed the test—the other didn't.

Before we get going, we need to take Oswalt's advice that, as with most Old Testament books, you and I need a basic knowledge of the historical background of the book of Isaiah to understand its message. This is so because God's revelation is mediated through a specific setting in time and space. While this may be out of our comfort zone, in the end there will be a big spiritual payoff, because Isaiah's truths will be put into the "concrete forms of daily life."[7]

What Oswalt is saying is that we have to do our homework and actually *study* the Word of God, which takes work (and means we need to get our maps out!). In Isaiah's case, unless we are satisfied with a few devotional/inspirational verses probably taken out of historical and exegetical context, we have to grasp the historical and geopolitical context. I think you would agree that if we put forth the effort, there are big spiritual dividends. So let's get our maps out and dig in!

With all this in mind, let's take a look at Isaiah 7–39, which showcases the theme of trust in God again and again. The big-picture issue is shall Israel/Judah trust the nations and political alliances or shall they trust in God? This problem is brought to focus in chapters 7–12 and 36–39, which are like bookends and are remarkably similar—two Judean kings facing overwhelming odds. One king trusted human power and political alliances; the other trusted God, although not completely.[8]

I love Oswalt's depiction of the tale of these two Judean kings: "Looking back over chapters 7–35 one gets the impression of looking at a programmed learning course. Ahaz was given a test . . . His choice was whether to trust God or Assyria."[9] Unfortunately, he

---

7. Oswalt, *Book of Isaiah*, 4.
8. Oswalt, *Book of Isaiah*, 55.
9. Oswalt, *Book of Isaiah*, 56.

struck out. Chapters 13–35 support the correct answer—God is to be trusted."[10]

Chapters 36–39 are the post-test. Again, a Judean king (Hezekiah) is put in a situation where he must trust God. Has he learned anything? Is he going to repeat his father's mistakes? No, he passes! He trusts God, who shows that he can be trusted.[11]

Let's go into some detail regarding these two kings because they will enrich our understanding of trust. Isaiah is a masterful poet and well worth our reading. King Ahaz of Judah (the southern kingdom)[12] seems to be a classic case study of someone who will not trust God. Assyria is now the superpower—the six-hundred-pound gorilla in the area that was flexing its military muscle[13]—so Syria and Israel (the northern kingdom),[14] which were like sitting ducks and in imminent danger of attack from Assyria, understandably try to forge an alliance with Ahaz. However, if that plan fell through, they would go to plan B and try to annex Judah and install a puppet king in place of Ahaz. However, Ahaz—not to be outfoxed—had his own plans and tried to buy off Tiglath-Pilesar III of Assyria with money to stave off an attack on his country.

---

10. Oswalt, *Book of Isaiah*, 56.

11. Oswalt, *Book of Isaiah*, 56.

12. The united kingdom of Israel under Solomon and David was divided into the northern and southern kingdoms in 930 BC. The northern kingdom is usually called Israel or Ephraim in the Old Testament, while the southern is called Judah.

13. Assyria (in what is now northern Iraq) was governed by a succession of weak rulers from about 823 to 745 BC. It was during this period that Assyria's neighboring countries enjoyed some measure of relief from Assyrian expansionism. Both Israel and Judah were no exceptions, and they enjoyed peace and prosperity not known since the days of Solomon. However, this was a false sense of security that the prophets Hosea and Amos were commissioned to disabuse the Israelite elites of—without much success. It was not until the accession of a ruler named Tiglath-Pileser III (his personal name was "Pul" as mentioned in 2 Kgs 15:19) in 745 that the period of Assyrian weakness was over. He made it well known that he intended to extend his dominion as far as possible—bad news for both Israel and Judah. See Oswalt, *Book of Isaiah*, 5–8 for details.

14. Israel, the northern kingdom, is also known as Ephraim.

Isaiah, in the midst of all this political intrigue, could not persuade King Ahaz to trust in Yahweh instead of geopolitical and military alliances. With biting metaphor Isaiah shows Ahaz he has nothing to fear from the kings of Israel and Syria. They are merely "two smoldering stumps of firebrands" (7:4 ESV). In other words, they were nobodies in terms of their geopolitical strength.

In 7:7, God announces that the Syro-Ephraimite coalition's violent plan would never happen. Until Ahaz really believes in God's sovereignty and can trust himself and his nation to God, he is doomed to continue living on the shaky political sands he is now living on (v. 2). Assyria will not offer true security. Only through trusting in the present and ultimate truth of God is any real security possible.[15] Verse 9b is worth quoting (and memorizing):

> If you are not firm in faith, you will not be firm at all.
> (ESV)

Sadly, Ahaz would not put God to the test (7:10–14) even though God himself gives Ahaz a golden opportunity to prove his trustworthiness. Listen to verse 10:

> Again the Lord spoke to Ahaz, "Ask a sign of the Lord your God; let it be deep as Sheol or high as heaven."
> (ESV)

In other words, God was apparently putting no limit on what Ahaz may ask. (How many *us* would like to be in this situation?) But Ahaz apparently already had his mind made up and appealed to piety, which, according to Oswalt can be a wonderful cover for unbelief. Oswalt also states that to the casual onlooker Ahaz did not appear to have too little faith, but rather *such a deep faith* that he did not want to look for evidence by putting God to the test. So he alludes to Scripture (Deut 6:16) out of context.[16]

However, Ahaz's statement is not born out of faith. If it were, he would have aborted his plans for an alliance with Assyria. Rather, it is lack of faith and unbelief that give rise to his

---

15. Oswalt, *Book of Isaiah*, 202.
16. Oswalt, *Book of Isaiah*, 203–6.

announcement. Ahaz has spiritual blinders that prevent him from believing God or putting God to the test. Ahaz is unwilling to take the risk and trust God.

So, Isaiah predicts disaster—*and disaster it is*:

> therefore, behold, the Lord is bringing up against them the waters of the River, mighty and many, the king of Assyria and all his glory. And it will rise over all its channels and go over all its banks, and will sweep on into Judah, it will overflow and pass on, reaching even to the neck, and its outspread wings will fill the breadth of your land, O Immanuel. (Isa 8:7–8 ESV)

Moving On in Isaiah

I would like to keep diving into the riches of Isaiah because he has so much to teach us about trusting God. The only way to get a handle on things is to study the rich tapestry of Isaiah's masterful poetry and prose.

Isaiah 9:8—10:4 is a carefully crafted poem of "uplifted-hand" oracles (9:12b, 17b, 21b; 10:4b) well worth our reading and one that answers a pressing theological question: how could Israel's political machinations against Judah come crashing down? Because of Assyria's superior military strength? Because of the coalition between Ahaz and Assyria? No, not according to Isaiah. Israel and, later, Judah must come to terms not with Assyria, but with God.

The take-home lesson is that the world is judged by God's moral standards, not by political, economic, or military strength. If Israel is taken down, it will be because she fails to live up to God's standards. It is not Assyria's anger to be feared, but God's.[17]

There are four stanzas, each one ending with, "For all this his anger is not turned away, and his hand is stretched out still" (ESV).

The people of Israel were facing the Assyrian threat and were trying to figure out how to deal with it. What this poem is saying is that Assyria is not the one with whom you have to come to terms— it is Yahweh. Although Israel was concerned with the Assyrian

---

17. Oswalt, *Book of Isaiah*, 249–50.

menace, Assyria was only a pawn in Yahweh's hand (10:5). Isaiah considers all peoples to be instruments of the sovereign God; he is present in and through the events of history. Although Assyria did not see herself a servant of Yahweh, she served God's purposes for a time and then was subject to the same judging God that chastised Israel. Therefore, God would destroy Assyria (a fire that will burn and devour, 10:16–19).[18, 19]

God tells Israel, "be not afraid of the Assyrians when they strike" (10:24b ESV), and to trust him because he will deal with Assyria and destroy her (10:24–34). These are encouraging words for us as we face the Assyrias of our lives.

God Is My Salvation

Now we come to one of the most beautiful songs in Scripture—thanksgiving to God and a wonderful reversal from the sorrowful Song of of the Vineyard of Isaiah 5:1–7, where God's chosen people (the choice vineyard) have become worthy of God's destruction. Isaiah 12 should be engraved into the hearts all believers.

> Behold, God is my salvation; I will trust, and will not be afraid; for the Lord God is my strength and my song, and he has become my salvation . . . Give thanks to the Lord, call upon his name, make known his deeds among the peoples, proclaim that his name is exalted. Sing praises to the Lord, for he has done gloriously; let this be made known in all the earth. (vv. 2–5 ESV)

Chapter 12 anticipates a time when the people will get it right and draw the right conclusions, the very ones Isaiah has

---

18. Oswalt, *Book of Isaiah*, 260–61.

19. Oswalt notes that Isaiah envisions a God who is not a prisoner of history—he is utterly transcendent. This truth is of unparalleled importance. Isaiah, although not the first to formulate it, may be the first to apply it to the historical process in a thoroughgoing way. Reading the book, one cannot come away without being impressed that God is unique and above all other so-called gods. He controls historical process according to his sovereign will. Chapters 40–46 exude God's sovereign nature.

been pressing for and the central focus of this Song of Trust—on a trustworthy God. This has been Isaiah's constant appeal (8:11–22). Isaiah was trying to get Ahaz to trust God, but Ahaz couldn't get his spiritual act together.[20]

But those who can trust the Lord will find that he indeed is their strength and their song, and he has become their salvation!

God on the World Stage

As mentioned above, Isaiah 13–35 functions to back up the claim that God is trustworthy. Isaiah shows us that God is the sovereign actor on the stage of history—Lord of the nations. No book on earth makes the case for trusting God more forcefully than Isaiah.[21] He presents us with oracles against Babylon (13:1—14:23) and Tyre (23:1–18), symbols of human sophistication, wealth, pride, glory and conquest. But they, too, are under God's judgment.[22]

Isaiah 27:12–13 is the climax of chapters 13–27 and reminds us of the glorious promises that the succeeding chapters serve to substantiate. These two verses most likely refer to that Great Day of the Lord at the consummation of all things. Listen to what Isaiah says:

> And in that day a great trumpet will be blown, and those who were lost in the land of Assyria and those who were driven out to the land of Egypt will come and worship the Lord on the holy mountain at Jerusalem. (Isa 27:13 ESV)

Glorious verses indeed! The vineyard that was discarded in Isaiah 5 is now transformed, tended and protected by God. It is now a "pleasant vineyard" . . . and the Lord its keeper, watered by God . . . filling the whole world with fruit" (Isa 27:2b–3a, 6b ESV), so that the whole world will "worship the Lord on the holy mountain at Jerusalem" (27:13b ESV).

20. Oswalt, *Book of Isaiah*, 291–92.
21. Oswalt, *Book of Isaiah*, 298.
22. Oswalt, *Book of Isaiah*, 427.

Isaiah 13–33 is brought to a powerful conclusion in chapters 34–35. To trust in this world is the ultimate folly. Chapter 34 reads a lot like Revelation; God punishes the earth with mind-boggling devastation. Isaiah's metaphoric language is severe, extreme, and graphic because God is enraged at the world and under his judgment. Isaiah is calling 911 because the world is hip-deep in idolatry and injustice and dead to God's law.

On the other hand, trusting in God puts his remnant in a garden of abundance, ultimate refreshment, and holiness. Isaiah 35 is one of the most beautiful chapters in Scripture. Meditate on Isaiah's words:

> The wilderness and the dry land shall be glad; the desert shall rejoice and blossom like the crocus; it shall blossom abundantly and rejoice with joy and singing . . . They shall see the glory of the Lord, the majesty of our God . . . For waters break forth in the wilderness, and streams in the desert; the burning sand shall become a pool, and the thirsty ground springs of water . . . And the ransomed of the Lord shall return and come to Zion with singing; and everlasting joy shall be upon their heads; they shall obtain gladness and joy, and sorrow and sighing shall flee away. (35:1–10 ESV)

The Post-Test

Now that Isaiah has made a powerful case for trusting in God, let's see how Hezekiah, the son of Ahaz, fares at crunch time. Chapters 36–39 are a lived-out historical object lesson that the nations are under God's sovereign control. It's no historical accident that Hezekiah is facing severe political and military pressure from the same nation as his father—Assyria.

Sennacherib, the king of Assyria, was knocking on the door of Jerusalem and with calm arrogance sent his man Rabshaqeh (the king's field commander) to get the job done. He was not there for a meet-and-greet. His goal was a takeover—their version of "shock and awe." His first tactic was some hardball arm-twisting.

His speech to Israel's leaders is a masterpiece of taunts, sophistry, and ultimatums, all coming from a hard-core idolator and polytheist. It is blasphemous toward the living God. He also provokes a theological crisis. If God is not sovereign, then Isaiah's words make no sense, and Assyria will win the day by brute force. [23]

Rabshaqeh's speech was probably X-rated—no words bleeped out. He used the crudest and most shocking terms he knew in an attempt to brutalize Israel. How's this for irony? Sennacherib even boasts that he more trustworthy than God, so all Judah has to do is trust this murderous egomaniac! (Isa 36:13–20).

But Sennacherib has made a fatal mistake—the Lord is a being of an entirely different order . . . not one among many gods. Jerusalem's fate has nothing to do with whether Sennacherib thinks he's the master of the universe or that he thinks his military machine can take any nation down. It has everything to do with the Lord, the only God (37:20).

For his part, Hezekiah couldn't stomach the living God being mocked, so he called for Isaiah, who (are we surprised?) told the king, "Do not be afraid because of the words that you have heard . . ." (37:6b ESV). Sound familiar? It's the same exhortation to trust God (7:4) that he gave Hezekiah's father, Ahaz, who miserably flunked the test of trust in God.

But God was not fazed by clueless despots like Sennacherib. All he had to do was put a spirit in him so that he heard a rumor and returned to Assyria, where he was killed (37:7, 38). Hezekiah went before the Lord and actually spread the Assyrian's blasphemous letter before the living God. Hezekiah's prayer shows his big concern was for the glory of God and "that all the kingdoms of the earth may know that you alone are the Lord" (37:20b ESV).

Note the order of things here. Sennacherib spoke to Hezekiah concerning the Lord; then Hezekiah spoke to the Lord concerning Sennacherib; now the Lord speaks to Hezekiah concerning Sennacherib. God has the last word and the one that counts. Sennacherib may have styled himself as world ruler, boasting of his scorched-earth devastation of other nations—but it is the

---

23. Oswalt, *Book of Isaiah*, 634.

sovereign God who will close the book on who Sennacherib really is, because it is God who rules Sennacherib (37:26–28).

If Sennacherib had bothered to do a background check on the Holy One of Israel, he may have discovered that another notorious tyrant met his match against this God. Pharaoh's mighty war machine got stuck in the mud of the Red Sea and they all "sank like lead in the mighty waters" (Exod 15:10 ESV). Pharaoh had to learn the hard way who is really on the throne (6:1–3).

Sennacherib boasts that nothing can stop him—he is the new bully on the block and had it all figured out. But God is not threatened by his war machine or his battle plans because he controls them. In fact, Sennacherib has been but a pawn in God's hand. Listen to what God says to the tyrant:

> Have you not heard that I determined it long ago? I planned it from days of old what I now bring to pass, that you should make fortified cities crash into heaps of ruins, while their inhabitants, shorn of strength, are dismayed and confounded, and have become like plants of the field and like tender grass, like grass on the housetops, blighted before it is grown. (Isa 37:26–27 ESV)

So God treats Sennacherib like a dumb ox made to do his master's bidding by stating, "I will put my hook in your nose and my bit in your mouth, and I will turn you back on the way by which you came" (37:29b ESV). What a rude awakening for the puffed-up despot! Jerusalem was miraculously delivered from his army when an angel of the Lord killed Assyrian soldiers—with a body count of a whopping 185,000 according to Scripture (37:36).

So, Sennacherib becomes a sort of poster child for world rulers who think they control things. When he went back home to Nineveh, he was executed with the sword by his own sons while worshipping in the house of his so-called gods (37:38). What an ignominious fall for the high and mighty—the price for mocking and blaspheming the living God.

By the way, Hezekiah passed the test of faith in God that Ahaz had failed. But are we really surprised that when his gut check was over he was seduced by this world's values: wealth, glory, luxury, arms? He dropped his guard when life was good and demonstrates for all of us that trust in God is not a "one and done" but a way of life. We need to cross the finish line.

I love dwelling on things like the glory, greatness, and trustworthiness of God. Exalting him and what he has done for us in Christ is fundamental to our ways as believers. But failing to trust God is part and parcel of our walk with God—who of us doesn't fall short at times? I certainly do. Look at Hezekiah: he passed the test of faith when the pressure was on, only to fail when life was good. He opened up a can of worms that had eternal consequences when he showed a Babylonian envoy (39:1–8) his treasury. It's like the United States giving Russia or North Korea all of our intellectual property or trade secrets. It made no sense for Hezekiah to show a pagan nation his temple vessels and material wealth. It was an act of the flesh and a failure to trust God. Ultimately, these same Babylonians carried off all this wealth back to Babylon after destroying Jerusalem and carrying the people of Israel into exile. All this after Jerusalem had just been miraculously delivered. What a turn in fortunes! How true it is:

> Pride goes before destruction. (Prov 16:18a NIV)

PART 3: GOD AND THE IDOLS

Before I close this chapter on trust in God, I would like to take a look at one attribute of God that is unique to him and that makes him utterly trustworthy: his relationship to time and his ability to know and predict the future. This is particularly Isaianic. That is to say, Isaiah is chock full of passages showing how God knows the future and controls it as the Lord of history. Isaiah's argument against idols depends heavily on Yahweh's ability to declare the future; if he can't, how can he be any better than idols?

Isaiah 41:21–29 sets up a court scene, with Yahweh asking the gods to present their case and bring their proof and tell us what is to happen—former things . . . that we may consider them . . . so we know they are gods ... and future things, so that we may know that they are gods. Listen to Isaiah's piercing prose:

> Set forth your case, says the Lord; bring your proofs, says the King of Jacob. Let them bring them and tell us what is to happen. Tell us the former things, what they are, that we may consider them, that we may know their outcome; or declare to us the things to come. Tell us what is to come hereafter, that we may know that you are gods; do good or do harm, that we may be dismayed and terrified. Behold, you are nothing, and your work is less than nothing; an abomination is he who chooses you. (41:21–24 ESV)

Those who trust in false gods should demand their money back, as Oswalt says. False gods cannot predict let alone bring about the future. But in verses 25–29 Yahweh, the "first and last," predicts that Cyrus, a pagan king would allow God's people to end their exile in Babylon and return to their homeland—an astonishing prediction.

Listen again to the precious promise that God gave Elaine on that miraculous weekend in 1979 when he led her to Isaiah 46:9–10 (TLB): "I clearly told you what was going to happen in the future. For I am God—I only—and there is no other like me who can tell you what is going to happen. All I say will come to pass, for I do whatever I wish."

Savor the beautiful doxology Daniel gives us of God's sovereign control over time and events:

> Blessed be the name of God forever and ever, to whom belong wisdom and might. He changes times and seasons; he removes kings and sets up kings; he gives wisdom to the wise and knowledge to those who have understanding; he reveals deep and hidden things; he knows what is in the darkness, and the light dwells with him. (Dan 2:20–22 ESV)

When Babylonian King Nebuchadnezzar pulled a fast one on his enchanters and diviners who were accustomed to consulting their manuals, they were no match for the God who controls history and reveals it to whom he wills. But Nebuchadnezzar finally got it right—after a degrading humiliation—when he blessed Almighty God:

> ... and he does according to his will among the host of heaven and among the inhabitants of the earth; and none can stay his hand or say to him, "What have you done?" (Dan 4:35b ESV)

His is not the testimony of a Bible-thumping Baptist but the then-most-powerful man on the earth, a pagan king who had to learn the hard way who was really in control of things.

The Bottom Line

We face many Assyrias in our modern-day world—threats knocking at our doors. Many people are uptight about what's going on in our world today. We know things are seriously out of whack. But if you believe our testimony of God's mighty hand working miracle after miracle in bringing about my transfer to Miami; if your heart resonates with Isaiah's powerful witness to the utmost faithfulness of the sovereign God; if you believe the testimonies of Daniel and Nebuchadnezzar, then you can trust this same triune God. There is no other sure foundation!

8

SALVATION

PART 1

It was that unforgettable Labor Day weekend of 1979. Elaine and I were hunkered down for Hurricane David, all boarded up in our house in Miami Springs, sitting on pins and needles, waiting for Ms. Binns to return from London. Then God gave us that very special verse:

> ... thus says the Lord to you. Do not fear or be dismayed ... for the battle is not yours but God's. Tomorrow go down against them . . . You need not fight in this battle; station yourselves, *stand and see the salvation of the Lord on your behalf* . . . do not fear or be dismayed; tomorrow go out to face them, for the Lord is with you. (2 Chr 20:15–17 NASB, emphasis added)

What a bombshell verse! There was so much in these verses impacting our situation. But as you can see from the text, this was a salvation experience. At that time I didn't bother questioning how that was possible because I was already "saved." Since then I have asked myself, "How was this a salvation experience?"

Again, running this experience through the Word of God and reading biblical scholars has given me some answers and has progressively transformed my view of salvation. The result has been a paradigm shift in the way I view redemption.

I accepted Jesus Christ as my Savior at the age of thirteen. I was at a summer camp for youth in Indiana. As the youth evangelist preached the message of personal salvation, I knew I was a sinner who needed a Savior, so I went forward and accepted Christ. That day is still crystal clear in my mind. Since then, I never questioned salvation as forgiveness of sins and going to heaven after death. It's what I heard in church. It's what I was taught in Sunday school and what I learned in one year of Bible college. It's what the Bible says, isn't it? It's still what I hear from the pulpit today.[1]

However, it wasn't until I enrolled in a Theology of Missions course in 1989 under Dr. Arthur Glasser mentioned in chapter 6 that things started to change. I was introduced to the concept of the kingdom of God in all its richness.

Like a breath of fresh air, I experienced vast new horizons regarding the kingdom and other important biblical themes. One was salvation. I learned that the kingdom is virtually synonymous with salvation and eternal life and that salvation is not just going to heaven but includes a present experience.

1. See Scott McKnight's book *The King Jesus Gospel* for a cogent critique of salvation culture preached in so many evangelical churches, one that focuses only on personal salvation. This, says McKnight, is not the original gospel. Another volume that is critical of the salvation culture in many evangelical churches is *Gospel Allegiance* by Matthew Bates. Bates thinks the current dominant approach to the gospel as a "transaction" to get people saved and on their way to heaven is reductionistic and only part of the gospel and seriously misses the royal and kingship aspects of the gospel that are part of the New Testament. As such, faith in Jesus is misunderstood and does not take into account total allegiance to Jesus as King. In reality, in this transaction model disciple-making can be problematic—a fringe benefit or icing on the cake. Also see *What Faith in Jesus Misses for Salvation in Christ* by Bates. In addition, he has a handy easy-to-read book designed for lay small groups, *The Gospel Precisely*. This small volume confronts truncated views of the gospel that leave out the kingship or messianic aspects of Jesus the Christ. Worth your reading.

The late Dallas Willard, in his book *The Great Omission*, makes a compelling case that contemporary American churches, while they may make converts, by and large do not make disciples. He states, "By not having made our converts disciples, it is impossible for us to teach them how to live as Christ lived and taught (Luke 14:26)." Willard, *Great Omission*, 6.

So the first stage in my transformed—and more biblical—understanding of salvation was that salvation is more than "fire insurance"—saving sinners from the eternal flames of hell so they can go to heaven. In other words, when God delivers us, heals us, or brings us into any kind of *shalom* before our final and complete redemption, these are also salvation experiences. So, when God brought Elaine and me from Guadalajara to Miami based on his prophetic promise, this was a kind of salvation experience. It aligned us with his will for our flourishing and benefit.

Heaven on Earth—The Bible's Big Secret

J. Richard Middleton, in *A New Heaven and a New Earth: Reclaiming Biblical Eschatology*, states that the Old Testament does not spiritualize salvation. It understands it as God's deliverance of people and land from all that destroys life and the restoration of both people and land to flourishing.[2] This sounds like a mouthful, but what he means is salvation is also concrete and earthy.

Therefore, salvation includes the redemption of nations and ultimately the entire created order. Amazingly, Middleton says this vision of God's goal to transform or redeem creation is perhaps the Bible's best-kept secret. More amazing is that this biblical view is unknown to most church members and even to many clergy.[3]

This holistic vision of salvation is rarely found in popular Christian piety or even in the liturgy of the church. Moreover, it is openly contradicted by many traditional hymns (and contemporary praise songs). The idea of an everlasting worship service in "our home beyond the skies" is a central theme in many hymns.[4] As the popular theologian and preacher A. W. Tozer is reputed to have said, "Christians don't tell lies; they just go to church and sing them."[5] Examples abound:

2. Middleton, *New Heaven and a New Earth*, 25.
3. Middleton, *New Heaven and a New Earth*, 24.
4. Middleton, *New Heaven and a New Earth*, 27–30.
5. Middleton, *New Heaven and a New Earth*, 29.

SALVATION

1. "Rock of Ages," written by Daniel Draper, an English Methodist. Third stanza: ". . . When I soar to worlds unknown, See Thee on Thy judgment throne . . ."
2. "Jesus, Keep Me Near the Cross," by Fanny Crosby.
   Third stanza: "Near the Cross, I'll watch and wait, hoping, trusting ever, Till I reach the golden strand, Just beyond the river."
3. "When the Roll Is Called Up Yonder."
   "On that bright and cloudless morning when the dead in Christ shall rise, And the glory of His resurrection share; When His chosen ones shall gather to their home beyond the skies, And the roll is called up yonder, I'll be there."
4. "The Old Rugged Cross."
   "Then he'll call me someday to my home far away, Where His glory forever I'll share."

I don't think Tozer was accusing hymns writers of intentionally misleading the faithful, and neither am I. But the idea of a heavenly home "up there" is so ingrained in evangelical Christianity that we can't imagine anything else. These hymns are a part of our Christian heritage. I grew up with them, love them dearly, and still sing them.

Fannie Crosby, who composed dozens of our beloved hymns, is one of the great saints of all time and has a crown of glory awaiting her. But we have to remember that these great hymns are not Scripture and, therefore, not inspired. Middleton correctly reminds us that people often learn much of their theology from songs and hymns, and this may be especially true about our eternal destiny, like "heaven."[6]

Unfortunately, for many of us churchgoers, salvation and eternal life still refer to going to heaven upon death. Middleton has actually had interviews conducted of Christians regarding the final destiny of believers. The answers are quite traditional, focusing on judgment and going heaven. Of course, "heaven" tends to

---

6. Middleton, *New Heaven and a New Earth*, 27.

be conceived as an unending worship service in God's immediate presence in another world.[7,8]

Redeeming Cosmos and Culture

But the shocker for me is that God's redemptive intent has always been to redeem the entire created order—*including human culture*—not just individual souls.

It's one thing for God to heal, deliver, and redeem people—quite another to redeem the cosmos (universe), nations, and culture. This is where Middleton's statement about redeeming and renewing creation being the Bible's best-kept secret is on target.

---

7. Middleton, *New Heaven and a New Earth*, 23

8. The idea of a heavenly destiny in an immaterial realm as the goal of salvation can be traced to the ancient Greek philosopher Plato (428–348/47 BC), who had a dualistic vision of reality that viewed the immaterial (intelligible) realm superior to the material (visible) world. With his famous theory of the "Forms," he believed that ultimate reality was not in concrete earthly existence but in the Forms, which function as perfect universal templates for everything we experience in the world. In the platonic scheme, therefore, matter is inferior to the spiritual.

So, for Plato the human soul is a prisoner of the body. This dualistic framework was given extra impetus by Roman philosopher Plotinus (AD 205–70), a Neoplatonist who had profound influence on the early church. Plotinus taught a hierarchical panentheism (everything is in God) through his theory of emanations. Things emanate from God the way rays emanate from the sun. Although the entire universe consists of God and his emanations, there is nevertheless a hierarchical arrangement, with the highest form of being the first emanation (nous or universal reason).

Salvation for Plotinus was spiritual ascent through moral and intellectual virtues without the distractions of the world. The goal was ecstatic union with the One. Neoplatonism had a profound influence on early Christian thinkers such as Augustine and spawned many Christian and non-Christian mystical movements that are still with us.

The idea of a transcendent, non-earthly realm as the final goal of salvation has been with us ever since. In other words, heaven as primarily a spiritual entity and the destiny of the saved, who will exist as spiritual beings engaged eternally in spiritual activity is syncretistic—a combination of biblical themes and the classical philosophical tradition.

When Middleton had his interviews done among believers, there was no conscious reflection on the redemption of human culture.[9]

I have to confess that I have been among many believers who have had inchoate ideas of a new heaven and a new earth and unsure how to put this into our framework of the afterlife. Middleton, on the other hand, has no such problem. He realizes that the Scriptures explicitly teach that God is committed to reclaiming creation (human and nonhuman) in order to bring it to its glorious destiny.

A couple of years ago I spent considerable time studying Isaiah. It's a majestic sixty-six chapters containing some of the most robust theology of God in the Bible. Isaiah also has a rich eschatology (theology of the future), with an emphasis on the future kingdom of Israel centered in Jerusalem—the place where God dwells with his people—where peace and righteousness reign. The prophet also gives us compelling images of God's commitment to transform and renew the created order (11:5–9; ch. 60; 65:17–25).

However, when I study Isaiah and other writing prophets, I notice a different emphasis between sermons I hear in church and the messages of judgment and restoration in the prophets. Evangelistic gospel sermons (at least the ones I hear) are almost always about individual salvation. Let me be clear: I think we all know that personal redemption is at at the heart of the gospel. Jesus came to save sinners like you and me. *People's* names are written in the Lamb's Book of Life. No doubt the fourth Servant Song in Isaiah 52:13—53:12 has in mind personal redemption. But Isaiah's concerns are also broader than sermons I typically hear.

Richard Mouw, in a wonderful treatment of Isaiah 60, says that some Christians have greatly emphasized the individual benefits of Christ's redemptive work and view his atonement (Jesus' work on the cross) almost exclusively in terms of a transaction that took place to secure the salvation of individuals.[10] He rightly notes that Christ's redemptive ministry is cosmic in scope. Jesus came to rescue a creation that was infected by the curse of sin—not limited

---

9. Middleton, *New Heaven and a New Earth*, 23.
10. Mouw, *When the Kings Come Marching In*, 106–7.

to human hearts, but touching the natural realm, *reaching into art, economics, and education* (italics added).[11] He believes we must share in God's desire for the renewal of the entire cosmos.[12]

Keeping in mind the sentiments of Mouw and Middleton, I cannot recall ever hearing a sermon about transformation of the created order or redemption of culture—themes prominent in the prophets (see above, plus Joel 3:17–18; Amos 9:11–15; Mic 4:1–5). If we believe the entire Bible is the authoritative Word of God, we must proclaim God's vision to renew all his creation, not just souls for heaven.

A More Biblical Vision of Salvation: Back to the Beginning

I agree with Middleton that many believers get off track and miss the boat and fail to understand the full-orbed nature of redemption and the final fulfillment of God's purposes because they have overlooked the overall plot structure of the Bible, especially its grounding in creation.

A lot of us read Scripture in piecemeal fashion; but unless we have a correct understanding of God's intention at creation, our entire view of redemption will be hopelessly off target. It makes sense to me that until we get it right and have a "clear grasp of the purpose and goal of earthly life (including how that purpose went off track), we will be at the mercy of unbiblical notions of salvation and eschatology."[13]

I confess that I have never found the traditional idea of an eternal disembodied choir service in heaven "up there" to be very interesting. However, my eyes have been opened to the brilliance of God's plan for transformation of his created order and our place in it with perfect fellowship with him. The work of contemporary biblical theologians is a breath of fresh air because they understand God's unswerving purpose to include the redemption of his

---

11. Mouw, *When the Kings Come Marching In*, 109.
12. Mouw, *When the Kings Come Marching In*, 111.
13. Middleton, *New Heaven and a New Earth*, 38–39.

creation and cosmos, rather than just whisk us off the earth to "up there."[14] They have opened up the biblical narrative that flows from Eden to the new Jerusalem and have shown the compelling inner logic of redemptive history in its fullness and beauty.

Back to the Drawing Board

So, I've had to go back to the drawing board in order to grasp what the Bible means by salvation and God's plans for his created order. To quote Lewis Carroll, we "begin at the beginning." That would be creation. I think there is plenty of scriptural evidence to support the assertion that God created the cosmos to glorify himself. Psalm 19:1 says, "The heavens declare the glory of God, and the sky above proclaims his handiwork" (ESV). To me it's plain that God is glorified in the natural world both at the macro level and micro level. Look at the stars at night... or study the complexities of the human body. What do you see?... the glory of God.

Earth Is God's Home

However, here's my concern. What is our role in how God glorifies himself? How do we fit in with God's glorification in the created order? As a starter, how many of us know that God created the earth as his temple/sanctuary?[15] Or that he designed it to be

---

14. Middleton, *New Heaven and a New Earth*, 57–58.

15. T. D. Alexander states that it is noteworthy that the garden of Eden is portrayed in Genesis as a divine sanctuary. The evidence rests largely on the striking parallels that exist between the garden and later Israelite sanctuaries—both were entered from the east and guarded by cherubim. In addition, the tabernacle menorah (lampstand) possibly symbolized the tree of life. It's significant that the Hebrew words for "serve" and "keep" used in God's command to the man to "work the garden and keep it" (Gen 2:15) are found in combination in the Pentateuch only in passages that describe the duties of the Levites in the sanctuary (priestly function). Alexander, *From Eden to the New Jerusalem*, 20–31.

In the series preface to Alexander's book *The City of God and the Goal of Creation*, 11, Ortlund and VanPelt note that although there have been great

a divine residence where he could coexist with humanity? This is the opinion of many modern scholars.[16, 17] T. D. Alexander posits that the garden in Eden is portrayed in Genesis as a divine sanctuary and cites John Walton, who states that "God does not set up the cosmos so that only people will have a place."[18] The earth was God's abode.

The opening chapters of Genesis imply that the boundaries of Eden would be expanded to fill the whole earth as we humans are fruitful and multiply. Over time, the entire earth would become a beautiful holy garden-city. Genesis 2 merely introduces the start of this process, but the goal is the establishment of a glorious temple-city where God and humanity coexist in perfect glory.[19]

G. K. Beale notes that God needed his human vicegerent (Adam) to extend the boundaries of God's presence worldwide. Adam's purpose in that first garden-temple (Eden) was to expand its boundaries until it circled the earth, so that the earth would be completely filled with God's glorious presence.[20] In other words, God created the earth to be his great temple/sanctuary—his home—but he needed us, his image-bearers, to "be fruitful and multiply" to spread that glorious presence.

Beale also notes that Adam, as priest-king in Eden, was to subdue the entire earth (Gen 1:28). Genesis 1:27 provides the means by which the commission and goal of verse 28 was to be accomplished—humanity would fulfill the mandate by means of being God's image-bearers, representing and reflecting his glorious presence. Because Adam and Eve were to subdue and rule "over all

---

advances in evangelical biblical scholarship over the past several generations with the recovery of biblical theology, most believers read the text piecemeal, "finding golden nuggets of inspiration here and there, but remain unable to plug any given text meaningfully into the overarching storyline." The renaissance of biblical theology is a blessing but, unfortunately, little of it has yet to make it to the average believer in the pew.

16. Alexander, *From Eden to the New Jerusalem*, 24.
17. Alexander, *From Eden to the New Jerusalem*, 25–26.
18. Alexander, *From Eden to the New Jerusalem*, 24.
19. Beale, *Temple in the Church's Mission*, 368–72.
20. Beale, *Temple in the Church's Mission*, 368–70.

the earth," it makes sense that they were to expand the geographical boundaries of the garden until Eden covered the whole earth. They were in the paradise of Eden, but outside of Eden lay a sort of no-man's-land, which had to be developed. They were in the first land developing business under God's sovereign rule. So their commission was to widen the boundaries of the edenic garden in ever-increasing circles into the same garden-temple they lived in.[21]

Let's make this matter easy—in nuts-and-bolts terms. The sacred presence of God, which was initially limited to the garden-temple of Eden, was to be extended throughout the whole earth by his image-bearers, as they themselves represented and mediated his holy presence.[22]

I think we are coming closer to answering my concern about our role in God glorifying himself in the cosmos. God is glorified as we, his image-bearers, "fill the earth" (1:18 ESV). However this filling is more than mere biological reproduction and diffusion of God's image-bearers over the earth. Middleton agrees that when the human race was commissioned to "fill the earth," this mandate implied more than having babies.[23]

God's Glory and the Cultural Mandate

However, we need to understand a critical dimension that appears in the Genesis account. For the destiny of creation to be fulfilled and God to be glorified, Adam was given dominion over the earth (Gen 1:26–28) and cultural power to subdue it. The Genesis narrative is clear: God created the human race to rule the earth. This kingly function is delegated, but it is real. Psalm 8:5–8 reads:

> Yet you have made him a little lower than the heavenly beings and crowned him with glory and honor. You have given him dominion over the works of your hands; you have put all things under his feet, all sheep and oxen, and

---

21. Beale, *Temple in the Church's Mission*, 81–83.
22. Middleton, *New Heaven and a New Earth*, 165.
23. Middleton, *New Heaven and a New Earth*, 165.

also the beasts of the field, the birds of the heavens, and the fish of the sea, whatever passes along the paths of the seas. (ESV)

God does not hoard power as sovereign ruler of the cosmos; rather, he assigns us a share in ruling the earth as his representatives (Gen 1:26–28). This delegation of power is seen in the fact that God, as Creator, assigns the freedom and responsibility to name the animals to man (Gen 1–2).[24]

So, I think it's safe to say that God does not micromanage the world. He expects us to rule and subdue the created order. The original human task in Genesis 2:15 is to work and protect the garden (which most scholars consider to be a priestly function).

In Psalm 8:5–8 humanity is entrusted with rule over animal life. Our vocation is earth oriented, involving the responsible exercise of human power on God's behalf over the non-human world. I take as a given that we are cultural creatures, assigned cultural power by God, and as we continue to multiply and increase we engage in cultural development. William Edgar states that the Bible teaches that cultural engagement before God is, along with worship, "the fundamental calling for the human race."[25]

Middleton believes that "ultimately the human vocation is a cultural mandate, grounded in agriculture, but including all forms of technological, societal, artistic and intellectual production . . . understood as our development of the originally pristine earth into a complex and beautiful civilization worthy of God's glory."[26] Put more simply, we, who live in God's cosmic temple (the earth), are meant to mediate God's presence into all the world by faithfully representing him in our cultural endeavors, as we rule the earth.[27] Heady stuff!

---

24. Middleton, *New Heaven and a New Earth*, 51.
25. Edgar, *Created and Creating*, 87.
26. Middleton, *New Heaven and a New Earth*, 60.
27. In a footnote, Middleton states that most Old Testament scholars interpret humanity's rule on God's behalf as precisely what Genesis 1:26–28 means by the "image" and "likeness" of God *(imago Dei)*. *A New Heaven and a New Earth*, 43. Middleton has an entire scholarly book devoted to the *imago Dei*,

Time-Out

Before I go any further, we need to take a time-out and say that our God-ordained rule over nature does not give us any right to trash the natural world. We are given a stewardship role over nature as we develop it. Our rule is delegated by the sovereign Lord and Creator of all, who loves his creation and "saw that it was good" (Gen 1:9, 12, 18, 21, 25, 31 ESV). We as Christians ought to care deeply about clean water, pollution, deforestation, biodiversity, and the climate. When I was in graduate school at Harvard University pursuing a master's degree in public health, I loved my courses in the environmental sciences and even took an amateur interest in environmental journalism, especially how environmental journalists interact with scientific data.

However, if anyone has a theological and theoretical basis for being concerned for the environment, it is the believer. We believe in the goodness of creation, as opposed to, say, a gnostic view of things, which sees matter as evil and creation as a mistake. I applaud evangelicals who are involved in environmental activism, although I acknowledge it can be politically polarizing. We as evangelicals, especially the older generations, have been negligent on environmental matters. If God cares for his creation, don't you think we should?

Moving On

Our royal task of exercising power to transform the earthly environment into a complex sociocultural world that glorifies the Creator (the cultural mandate) is a holy task, a sacred calling. This cultural power over creation is modeled on God's own exercise of creative power—nonviolent and celebrating the goodness of creation. This will be completed in the new heaven and new earth

---

titled *The Liberating Image*. In it, he concludes that careful exegesis of Genesis 1:26–28, along with intertextual reading of the symbolic world of Genesis 1, suggests that *imago Dei* refers to human rule, the exercise of power on God's behalf in creation.

at the consummation of all things.[28] To me this has been nothing short of revolutionary.

God's plan at creation was to delegate power and authority to us as his vice-kings and give us priestly functions to care for his creation and to give us the privilege of developing the earth to his glory. Edgar reminds us that Genesis tells us the world God made was exceedingly good but not perfect. There was room for improvement.[29] We had a mandate to exercise cultural power to rule and subdue the earth until it, as God's temple, is filled with his glory.

However, Adam spoiled it all by disobeying this mandate, so that humanity no longer enjoyed God's presence in the garden. Therefore, all human efforts to extend God's glorious presence throughout a sinful earth have met with limited success at best.

PART 2

God's Plan to Move Forward

When Adam and Eve were kicked out of the garden from God's presence, people continued to live on the earth. But God's special revealing presence was now associated with heaven, until he entered into a covenant with Israel at Sinai and dwelled in the midst of humanity once again in the Israelite camp in the tabernacle, especially in the holy of holies.[30] God was moving forward with his plan to dwell with his people.

Many of us are ignorant about the tabernacle and find it boring. On the contrary, it's quite fascinating. The tabernacle was where God dwelled with Israel. It's also where sacrifices occurred. But few of us may know that it was also a mini-model of creation, with the garden of Eden as it's prototypical temple where God first dwelled with his people. Beale believes that the Old Testament tabernacle, as a microcosmic symbolic structure, was intentionally

---

28. Middleton, *New Heaven and a New Earth*, 49, 51, 60.
29. Edgar, *Created and Creating*, 56.
30. Alexander, *From Eden to the New Jerusalem*, 15.

designed to point to the cosmic future reality that was to be extended throughout the whole earth. In plain words, the tabernacle was intentionally designed to be a symbolic architectural structure of creation that pointed ahead to the final temple of Revelation 21–22, when God's glorious presence fills the entire earth.[31]

Although I won't go into meticulous detail (the reader is referred to Beale's *Temple in the Church's Mission*), it's really neat to observe how intricately the tabernacle and, later, Solomon's temple were patterned after God's creation of the cosmos and the edenic temple/sanctuary. Construction of the tabernacle was a big step toward the fulfillment of God's plan that the earth should become his dwelling place. The tabernacle had features that would recall the garden of Eden, such as its structure and furnishings. It was not only the locus of God's special presence but was designed to remind the Israelites (and us) of God's original purpose for the world—that the whole earth should become his dwelling place.[32]

Since God's creation project is to create a temple-city that will fill the whole earth, it is easy to see how Jerusalem is viewed as partially fulfilling God's plan. Jerusalem/Zion is a model of God's creation blueprint and reflects in microcosm what God intends for the earth. As the dwelling place of God on earth, the temple-city of Jerusalem is in miniature what God intends for the whole world. However, it is not the final product.[33] The temple was a symbolic reminder that one day God's glorious presence would fill the cosmos.[34]

In a sense the Old Testament story climaxes with the construction Solomon's temple, which was a magnificent structure. But both moral and spiritual failure by Israel's kings and citizens led to the destruction of God's city and temple and exile to Babylon. Israel repeatedly fell below God's moral standards necessary for living in the presence of God. All one has to do is read Isaiah's harsh condemnation of God's people in Isaiah 1:1–4:

31. Beale, *Temple in the Church's Mission*, 25–26.
32. Beale, *Temple in the Church's Mission*, 23–26.
33. Alexander, *From Eden to the New Jerusalem*, 31–42.
34. Alexander, *From Eden to the New Jerusalem*, 42.

> Hear, O heavens, and give ear, O earth; for the Lord has spoken: Children I have reared and brought up, but they have rebelled against me. The ox knows its owner, and the donkey its master's crib, but Israel does not know, my people do not understand. Ah, sinful nation, a people laden with iniquity, offspring of evildoers, children who deal corruptly! They have forsaken the Lord, they have despised the Holy One of Israel, they are utterly estranged. (ESV)

Ouch!

Jerusalem to the New Jerusalem

From this point, God moves forward in perhaps an unexpected direction. For example, Isaiah sees the future transformation of Jerusalem. His vision moves from the historical Jerusalem of the eighth century (under judgment) to the Jerusalem of the future age, which is the center of the new cosmos. To this new Jerusalem the nations come (66:18–21; 60:1–22) so that ultimately they find their salvation in Zion. The new Jerusalem is thus a symbol of the new creation.

You will notice that Zion/Jerusalem is now central to Old Testament eschatology. The prophets anticipated a future transformed city of Jerusalem that goes far beyond a mere restoration of the city to its pre-exilic glory—a radically different future. This expectation brings to fulfillment God's creation blueprint, for it anticipates the Lord's dwelling in a temple-city that will fill the whole earth. Many passages in Isaiah contribute to this future hope, but 65:17–25 is perhaps one of the most significant (and beautiful):

> For behold, I create new heavens and a new earth, and the former things shall not be remembered or come to mind. But be glad and rejoice forever in that which I create; for behold, I create Jerusalem to be a joy, and her people to be a gladness. I will rejoice in Jerusalem and be glad in my people. (65:17–19a ESV)

However, the next stage in the biblical meta-story introduces an important transformation that involves the replacement of the Jerusalem temple by a new and very different edifice.[35] This next—and crucial—step is intimately linked to the redemptive incarnation of Jesus Christ—the final Adam, in whom temple and body are united—and to the church, the body of Christ. The New Testament presents Christ's own body as a temple. Since he is the temple of God, Paul reminds us that we, as believers, who are "in Christ" as the body of Christ, are also the temple of God (1 Cor 3:16–17).

The creation of the church as a dwelling place of God involves a subtle but significant shift in emphasis. Whereas in the Old Testament God was perceived as dwelling *among* his people, in the New Testament he is viewed as dwelling *within* his people.

Although the church, as God's dwelling place—with its expansion of God's presence from Jerusalem to the ends of the earth—plays an important role in partially realizing God's creation blueprint for the earth, it, too, like the Jerusalem temple, has limitations. For the ultimate realization of God's purposes for the world we must look to the new Jerusalem of Revelation of 21–22.

The Final Act in God's Plan

The Bible begins with a garden and ends with a city. Revelation ends with a fascinating vision:

> Then I saw a new heaven and a new earth, for the first heaven and the first earth had passed away, and the sea was no more. And I saw the holy city, new Jerusalem, coming down out of heaven from God, prepared as a bride adorned for her husband. And I heard a loud voice from the throne saying, 'Behold, the dwelling place of God is with man. He will dwell with them, and they will be his people, and God himself will be with them as their God. (Rev 21:1–3 ESV)

---

35. Clowney, quoted in Alexander, *From Eden to the New Jerusalem*, 71.

You will notice that there is a marvelous continuity between Eden and the new Jerusalem, which is a gigantic solid-gold cubic analogue of the holy of holies of the tabernacle and temple. It also has unmistakable garden-like elements of Eden integrated into it, such as such as the tree of life and the river of the "water of life." However, the biggest aspect of continuity is God's presence—both are places of his sacred presence. In both, he coexists with us, his image-bearers.

John depicts the glorious grand finale of a trajectory found throughout Scripture—the intended destiny of heaven and earth as the final cosmic temple—God's sacred dwelling. Genesis presents the earth as a garden/temple brimming with potential—waiting to be filled with his glorious presence. John's vision gives us the finished product—a gigantic temple-city overflowing with God's glorious presence.

Eden and the new Jerusalem are like matching bookends, framing the entire biblical meta-story. But the theme is the same: God filling creation with his glorious presence and dwelling on earth with his people.

As golden cubes, the holy of holies and the new Jerusalem are clearly connected. God dwells inside both of these structures. To me, it seems that the entire new Jerusalem is a vastly expanded holy of holies. Revelation 21:18 (ESV) says the city-temple will be "pure gold, like clear glass." The entire holy of holies of Israel's temple, which was paved with gold on the walls, floor, and ceiling, has been expanded to cover the entire earth. This is why 21:16 says the whole city is cubic—because the holy of holies was such a shape.

John's vision articulates a breathtaking "mission accomplished" picture. When the new Jerusalem descends from heaven, God's presence decisively shifts from heaven to earth. That's why in the next verse a loud voice from God's throne declares, "Behold, the dwelling place of God is with man. He will dwell with them, and they will be his people, and God himself will be with them as their God" (Rev 21:3 ESV). The center of God's rule of the cosmos from now on will be permanently established on a renewed and transformed earth. The destiny of God's cosmic temple is now complete.[36]

The consummation of all things is accomplished and "the earth shall be full of the knowledge of the Lord as the waters cover the sea" (Isa 11:9b ESV). Once again God will dwell with us and we will be his people, and he will be our God! (Rev 21:3). Our salvation will be complete.

One Final Note

Imagine—one prophetic experience four decades ago has had a wondrous spiritual cascading effect on me and led me to the glorious riches of God's sovereign blueprint for his creation, that he might dwell with us forever on earth as our God and reign forever over his creation. To God be the glory!

---

36. Middleton, *New Heaven and a New Earth*, 170.

9

SEEING GOD

SIGHT UNSEEN

ONE OF THE UNFORESEEN effects of my prophetic experience is my captivation with what is known as the "beatific vision." In short, it means seeing God's face. This may sound like Greek to many, but bear with me. The beatific vision has a long Christian tradition in the church, especially in the church fathers and the Catholic Church. Unfortunately, it has been all but lost to modern evangelicals. However, before you buy me a one-way ticket to the nearest medieval monastery, let me explain.

In our modern world there is what moral philosopher Charles Taylor calls a "suffocating immanence," even among believers.[1] In other words, today's secularism has swallowed up almost any sense of transcendence that we might have. That's why talk of seeing God probably sounds too weird or otherworldly for most of us—we just don't talk this way. We feel comfortable talking about how God helps us with our finances, families, marriages, careers—all to the glory of God. We all want to follow Jesus and "make much of him," but few words are spoken of experiencing the idea of supreme blessedness in God's presence . . . of seeing him face-to-face. I don't

---

1. Quoted in Smith, *How (Not) to Be Secular*, 3.

see many church members prostrating themselves before a holy and majestic God. It's all but lost. We live in what Taylor calls the "immanent frame,"[2] that is, the here and now. But if I read the apostle Paul correctly, we are to set our minds on the things above, where Christ is, at the right hand of God (Col 3:1–2).

Even though the vision of God has had a strong emphasis in Roman Catholic theology, it has been sidelined in modern Protestant and evangelical circles. (Mention it to an evangelical friend of yours and see the blank look you get.) But the idea is of profound importance to our hope in Christ. Jesus, in the Beatitudes, tells us, "Blessed are the pure in heart, for they shall see God" (Matt 5:8 ESV).

This blessedness of gazing on God in Christ I see as the utmost joy—the fulfillment of our Christian walk. John explicitly mentions the beatific vision in Revelation 22:4–5, where he says that the saints will see God's face, "for the Lord God will be their light, and they will reign forever and ever" (ESV).

Four decades ago I heard (and saw) God's voice; now I want to see his face and experience his joy and blessedness. This is profoundly biblical with a long scriptural pedigree. As I have struggled to understand my desire to gaze upon God and experience his supreme happiness and how to put it into words, I have found the writing of Hans Boersma helpful. His book *Seeing God* has been instrumental in helping me with the theology of the beatific vision—allowing me to put my desire into words.

Due to the influence of Boersma, I now have a sacramental view of reality—all of reality, including the cosmos. This also has had implications on how I view Communion and the church. I have no plans to convert to Roman Catholicism or Eastern Orthodoxy—but this chapter will explain a seismic shift in my spiritual thinking.

When I say that I have a sacrament view of reality (ontology), I mean that we (and all of reality) participate in the divine life. Doesn't Paul say as much in Acts 17:28 when he states, "In him we live and move and have our being" (ESV)? It's not that the heavens

---

2. Quoted in Smith, *How (Not) to Be Secular*, 4.

merely declare the glory of God and declare his handiwork (Ps 19:1), but there is a close *participatory* (sacramental) link between earthly and heavenly realities. This may be hard to grasp, but let's try a little thought experiment: What if God ceased to exist? What would happen to the world and to us as his creatures? Would we continue to exist? I think many of us have a gut feeling that we can't exist without God—that we are not self-existent beings. Only God is that kind of being. So, it seems logical somehow that the earthly participates in the heavenly.

Participation in the divine life is not our (evangelical) default way of thinking—it seems strange to us. However, because of complicated historical and cultural developments,[3] it's not foreign to Orthodox Christians, who have a sacramental view of life, where union with and even partaking of the divine nature (divinization or "theosis") is the ultimate goal of salvation (see 2 Pet 1:4).[4] Some may think this sounds a bit like heresy because it seems to erase the Creator-creature distinction, but it does not. It's just not part of our Western theological heritage for the most part.

20/20 VISION?

What does it mean to see God, especially to see his face? Are we talking about literally seeing him, or is this about a spiritual vision of God? Sight is a vital sense to us humans. Loss of vision can be devastating. What is it about seeing God's face that is so important?

When our kids were growing up, our family would often take trips to Orlando, which is only about a two-hour drive from our home in the West Palm Beach area. I remember one event when I was in a large outdoor pool at a hotel near Sea World with all five

---

3. See Boersma, *Heavenly Participation*, especially part 1, for a detailed account of the historical, theological, and cultural factors that led to the world we live in now, i.e., one that is void of mystery and and sacramental mindset.

4. S. T. Kimbrough Jr. documents that Charles Wesley's thinking on salvation was saturated with the idea of participation in the divine nature. This has major implications for spiritual formation in Wesleyan theology and in ecumenical conversation. Kimbrough, *Partakers of the Divine Life*.

of our kids. Since I wasn't wearing my glasses in the pool—and was blind as a bat without them—I was unable to see my own kids in the pool. (I had been nearsighted since third grade.) So, I became fed up with being four-eyed and decided to have LASIK surgery. A few months later, I will never forget coming out of the microkeratome (the machine that sculpts the cornea with micro-precision) with new eyes and perfect vision without glasses! Is this how we are going to see God—with 20/20 vision?

Is the vision of God our ultimate end or telos? Quite possibly. Is it also a metaphor? I tend to think so, because Scripture is loaded with a dizzying number of poignant images trying to describe the reality of the future age. No one metaphor can portray that reality, so we have to piece them together like a jigsaw puzzle to make sense of the glory that is to be ours. Language cannot do justice to our eschatological (future) relationship with God. This is not a negative thing. Metaphors are the stuff of which human language is made, and they allow us to make sense of the world around us. Our access to God is indirect because he is utterly transcendent in his being.

Nevertheless, it is important to me to know that we are promised to see God's face (Rev 22:4 ESV). I anticipate seeing him at the end of my life and especially at the end of history.

That being said, Boersma has led me to Anselm of Canterbury (1033–1109), a medieval theologian, who is a prime example of someone whose deepest desire is to see God. But he struggles with the question of how to move from the world of sight and sound to the transcendent realm of God. At times he seems to despair of ever entering into the divine light, since he has never seen God and does not even know what to look for. But seeing God is the purpose for which he has been created, so he embarks on a quest for that final end for which he is made: the beatific vision.[5] I can relate to Anselm's prayers, which are recorded in his *Proslogion*.[6] Sometimes my own vision of God seems so dim that I think I'm spiritually blind. The "cares of the world" (Matt 13:22)

---

5. Boersma, *Seeing God*, 23.
6. Anselm, *Prayers and Meditations*.

choke off any vision of God that I may have, and I can only utter with Anselm,

> Come now, little man, turn aside for a little while from your daily employment, escape for a moment from the tumult of your thoughts. Put aside your weighty cares, let your burdensome distractions wait, free yourself awhile for God and rest awhile in him.[7]

We need to be patient because our earthly contemplation of God is only a provisional way of seeing him—a sneak preview. The ultimate beatific vision of God awaits us in the new heaven and new earth. Our earthly journey is a pilgrimage, a learning curve, in which God indwells us through his Spirit and unites us to Christ. As an "inner teacher" he guides us along the process of salvation and accustoms us to seeing him, so that our vision of him improves over time.[8]

However, our pilgrimage in this life is already a participation in the life of God and, as such, already a vision of God . . . but cannot compare to the final beatific vision of God in Christ.[9] Boersma is correct when he states that our Christian walk is still transformative, making us more Christlike as God gives us a greater vision of himself in Christ.[10]

Scripture says that without holiness no one will see God (Heb 12:14), so this transforming process is unique. In him, we join the divine life, becoming sons of God (Rom 8:14–17; Gal 4:4–7). This Christian teaching of divinization does not mean that we take the place of God . . . but we are transformed into the likeness of the object our vision; we are changed so as to become more like God in Christ.[11]

More verses come from the pen of the apostle Paul, who states, "And we all, with unveiled face, beholding the glory of the Lord, are being transformed into the same image from one degree

---

7. Ward, trans., *Prayers and Meditations of Saint Anselm*, 52.
8. Boersma. *Seeing God*, 388–89.
9. Boersma, *Seeing God*, 391.
10. Boersma, *Seeing God*, 393.
11. Boersma, *Seeing God*, 393.

of glory to another..." (2 Cor 3:18a ESV). In other words, the glory of God becomes ours, so that, like God—and the risen Christ—we take on incorruptibility and immortality (1 Cor 15:53–54). So, to become "partakers of the divine nature" (2 Pet 1:4 ESV) means that we escape the "corruption" of the world as we share increasingly in the divine virtues. Peter claims that God calls us to his own "glory and excellence" (2 Pet 1:3 ESV), and immediately after mentions our participation in the divine nature and our escape from corruption, then spells out in detail how these "excellences" and "virtues" of the divine nature take shape in the human life of virtue (1:5–7).[12] To me, this is exciting—thinking of the future that God has in store for us believers. No wonder Paul could say that no one could imagine what God has prepared for those who love him (1 Cor 2:9).

CONCLUDING REMARKS

Some have thought that the beatific vision implies an endless static vision of God—merely staring at God forever. I think this is a gross caricature of what God has in store for us. Boersma mentions the remarks of theologian Balthasar, who believes that all the elements that contribute to the perfections of true communion, which is seen in the blessed Trinity—self-surrender, creativity, receptivity, mystery—must be aspects of the beatific vision. This Trinitarian dynamism precludes the possibility of eternal life being reduced to mere static contemplation of the divinity.[13] I could not agree more.

Although communion with God is at the core of eternal life, this does not prevent us from carrying over our cultural accomplishments and activities and social lives into the new heaven and new earth any more than it does in this age.[14] God created us as cultural beings; this will be no less true in the next age.

---

12. Boersma, *Seeing God*, 394.
13. Boersma, *Seeing God*, 30–31.
14. Boersma *Seeing God*, 33, 39.

Theologian Bavinck thinks there can be both culture and contemplation in the eschaton: "The service of God, mutual communion, and inhabiting the new heaven and new earth undoubtedly offer abundant opportunity for the exercise of these offices (priest, king), even though the form and manner of this exercise are unknown to us."[15]

Perhaps our bodily resurrection should clue us in that our vision of God will be physical. Maybe we should take seriously that we will see God with physical eyes. Boersma gives us a tantalizing suggestion that maybe our physical sight will not so much be replaced by spiritual sight as it will be transformed into spiritual sight without ceasing to be physical. God may transform both the physical senses and the intellect, so that the entire human person is elevated to a higher level by the Spirit and at this level engages in ecstatic communion with God![16] Perhaps our sense of pleasure of both God and creation will be transformed to levels we cannot now comprehend in the hereafter by God. In this life we often associate intense pleasure with too much indulgence or extravagance because we live in a fallen world. But in an unfallen state this may not be the case—rich and sustained sensory delights may be right. This point is implied by C. S. Lewis in *Perelandra*.[17]

Whatever Revelation 22:4 ultimately means when it says we will see God's face, I'm sure that the sparkling metaphors that Scripture uses cannot match the reality to come of enjoying the eternal blessed presence of the triune God, for which this life is but a dress rehearsal. But the beatific vision, at its best, is a scintillating biblical metaphor that reflects a reality that ultimately is hard to wrap the mind around.

Though I have been privileged to see God's voice, I have to admit that my understanding and vision of God in Christ is still frustratingly incomplete. I, too, "see through a mirror dimly" (1 Cor 13:12a ESV). But I know that in the not too distant future I will see the unparalleled beauty of this same God. I will see his

---

15. Boersma, *Seeing God*, 40.
16. Boersma, *Seeing God*, 424.
17. Lewis, *Perelandra*, 33–38.

face. Again, I can't beat Anselm when it comes when it comes to expressing my longings. Listen to the unsurpassed beauty of his prayer:

> My God, I pray that I may so know you and love you that I may rejoice in you. And if I may not do so fully in this life, let me go steadily on to the day when I come to that fullness... Let me receive that which you promised through your truth, 'that my joy may be full.' God of truth, I ask that I may receive, so that my joy may be full.
> Meanwhile, let my mind meditate on it,
> > let my tongue speak of it,
> > let my heart love it,
> > let my mouth preach it,
> > let my soul hunger for it,
> > let my flesh thirst for it
> > let my whole being desire it,
>
> until I enter into the joy of my Lord, who is God one and triune, blessed forever. Amen.[18]

---

18. Ward, trans., *Prayers and Meditations of St. Anselm*, 266–67.

PART 2

INTRODUCTION—PROPHETIC CONSCIOUSNESS AND CALLING

THE FIRST PART OF this book, although quite lengthy and detailed, describes a prophetic journey in the sense that God spoke to me in two prophetic visions predicting the future. Elaine and I saw these predictions play out. Part 2 of this book also involves the prophetic but in a different way.

I was called by God to a prophetic task to deliver a message to people in positions of influence. The second part of the book will be much shorter—only two chapters. The first chapter will attempt to describe prophetic consciousness—what does a prophet think and feel? Here I make no authoritative claims. But I have to wonder if what I experienced when I saw the voice of God was the same kind of experience that some of the Old Testament prophets had (see Amos 1:1, for example). Most likely, if you had had the same experience as I, you would wonder the same thing. The prophets are fascinating but hard to understand, so I try to get a handle (as best I can) on how they perceived things and how this relates to the prophetic task that God gave me.

The second chapter of Part 2 will detail the prophetic task given me by God. The story is complicated but I offer a barebones sketch of it with no names or institutions named. In other words, I will be as generic as I can be without losing a sense of the narrative structure that is necessary to provide a context. I have no grudges or scores to settle and wish no harm to anyone involved in the story. My goal is simply to provide a context for a contemporary prophetic task and to glorify God with that narrative. Writing the narrative was not especially easy for me because I took no delight in the task. In some ways, it's painful to recall the events—but they happened and they are a part of who I am and the way God made me. For this I can and should offer no apologies.

10

CAN WE WRAP OUR MINDS AROUND THE PROPHET?

The biblical prophets may be the most misunderstood and mysterious men and women to those of us who live in the digital age. They are often lumped together as "the prophets" even thought they are vastly different in their audiences, styles, and messages. I have heard people in our church ask how God spoke to "the prophets." I take this to mean they had little idea how God would communicate to people like Isaiah and Ezekiel.

Prophecy is also widely misunderstood. Many of us, when we think about prophecy, think about the rapture, the latest geopolitical events in the Middle East, stockpiling supplies for the apocalypse, etc. So, with all these things in mind, my aim is to make the prophets less mysterious and more understood.

Certainly, prophets were called by God to a task to proclaim a prophetic word, but what about their consciousness? What were they thinking and feeling? Is it possible to get inside their heads? Unfortunately, the only prophet who gives us any significant insight into his inner life is Jeremiah, who is called the "weeping prophet" (Jer 13:17 ESV).

What sort of person was the prophet? Would they spook us? Were they loners? Sociable? Or were they aloof and weird . . . even disturbed? Were they all doom and gloom? Are people born with an innate prophetic bent? These are questions we might want to answer—if we can.

God called them to a ministry that was not easy. Many of them did not even want to be a prophet because the task was so demanding and unpopular. That's why God had to make Ezekiel's face hard as flint (Ezek 3:7–9)—so "whether they hear or refuse to hear (for they are a rebellious house) they will know that a prophet has been among them" (Ezek 2:5 ESV).

First of all, I think we need to get it straight that the main job of a prophet was not foretelling or predicting the future (certainly they also did that) but forth-telling. This means they proclaimed a word from God, often of divine judgment on injustice and idolatry. But they matched God's wrath with words of divine compassion and grace. Predictions of disaster were calls to repentance. The prophets had lots of doom and gloom, but they also preached abundant hope based on repentance. Read the book of Isaiah, for example, and you will see it filled with God's grace toward his rebellious people.

However, let's fast-forward to today's modern world. Are things any different? Are there still corruption and injustice? To be sure. But, although most of us are aware of corruption and injustice in the world around us and may be even cynical about our own government and politicians, we go on with our daily lives without making many waves. We just assume that's the way the world is. To us, cheating in business, exploiting the poor, is "just the way things are."

But to the prophet things were different. It's not that corruption, social injustice, and idolatry were any worse in Old Testament Israel. (Can anything be worse than what investigative correspondent Tom Burgis describes in his book *Kleptopia*,[1] in which he exposes the stunning extent of global corruption and dirty money that run like a river of sewage around the world?)

So, why all the indignation and outrage? Are the prophets overreacting? Abraham Heschel says that the things that horrified the prophets are now daily occurrences all over the world, and

---

1. Burgis, *Kleptopia*.

states that there is no society to which Amos's words would not apply.²

> Hear this, you who trample on the needy and bring the poor of the land to an end, saying "When will the new moon be over, that we may sell grain? And the Sabbath, that we may offer wheat for sale, that we may make the ephah small and the shekel great and deal deceitfully with false balances, that we may buy the poor for silver and the needy for a pair of sandals and sell the chaff of the wheat?" (Amos 8:4–6 ESV)

Heschel says that their breathless impatience with injustice may strike us as hysteria and that although we may witness acts of injustice, hypocrisy, and misery, we rarely grow indignant or overly excited. To the prophets, however, even a minor injustice assumed cosmic proportions.³ "They speak and act as if they sky were about to collapse because Israel has become unfaithful to God."⁴

SO, WHAT'S THE BIG DEAL, AMOS?

Amos is a good case study for us. He was a farmer from the southern kingdom who was called to minister to Samaria, capital of the northern kingdom. At that time there was affluence in Samaria, and the upper class flourished. There were no political or military enemies to deal with. Life was good—lavish houses, fine food and wine—all the best.

But Amos sees beyond all the glitz and glamour and develops a brilliant strategy to get Samaria's attention: he develops a laundry list of the sins of Israel's neighboring pagan nations, starting at the periphery and then moving inward, with the last nation Judah—a sort of "reverse ripple" strategy. He calls out the human rights violations of these nations: barbarism, slavery, promise-breaking, hatred and atrocities. They're all there. You can almost see the

---

2. Heschel, *Prophets*, 3.
3. Heschel, *Prophets*, 4.
4. Heschel, *Prophets*, 5.

Samarians patting themselves on the back in smug self-righteousness at the sins of the other nations. But as the noose of God's judgment begins to tighten by indicting the sister nations of God's chosen people, things get a little uncomfortable. "Hey, Amos, you're coming too close to home," they may have been thinking.

Amos then attacks the northern kingdom, as God comes as a roaring lion, ready to devour. God's people have not lived up to covenant standards; they have sinned against grace. Coveting, religious hypocrisy, oppression, and unrestricted self-advantage are rampant. People of the northern kingdom are busy economically and religiously—lots of buying, selling, religious festivals, prayers, and piety. But God is not faked out by their religiosity because their hearts are far from him. So he is busy too: sending drought, famine, and epidemics.

A visitor to Samaria back then might have been wowed by the fine houses, impressive buildings, and temples, but Amos was not impressed by all that the world values and worships and focuses on the oppression and exploitation. All the splendor was tainted by moral decadence.

> I abhor the pride of Jacob and hate his strongholds.
> (Amos 6:8a ESV)

The world has always worshipped power and wealth. But listen to what Jeremiah says:

> Thus says the Lord: "Let not the wise man boast in his wisdom, let not the mighty man boast in his might, let not the rich man boast in his riches, but let him who boasts, boast in this, that he understands and knows me, that I am the Lord who practices steadfast love, justice and righteousness in the earth. For in these things I delight, says the Lord." (Jer 9:23-4 ESV)

SEEING THINGS GOD'S WAY

The prophets make a big deal about the poor not getting a fair shake, about cheating in business, and about God not getting his fair due. Why are they scandalized about such things? We all know the world is a messy place, so why don't they just accept it like the rest of us? I think part of the answer is that they see the world from God's perspective, not man's.[5]

Heschel makes this point and believes this gives them a deep sensitivity to evil that we may perceive as hysterical. Heschel also keenly observes that if we think the prophet's rebuke is hysterical or obsessed, what should we call the abysmal indifference he confronts and which he bewails?[6] Listen to Amos's stinging indictment:

> Woe to them who lie on beds of ivory and stretch themselves out on their couches, and eat lambs from the flock . . . who sing idle songs to the sound of the harp . . . who drink wine in bowls and anoint themselves with the finest oils, but are not grieved over the ruin of Joseph! (Amos 6:4–6 ESV)

God hates sin. The prophets, too. So should we, although we don't—at least not like we should.

CALLING IT LIKE IT IS

Because the prophets see things from God's perspective, they call sin what it is and challenge evasions, fudges, excuses, head-in-the-sand posturing, scapegoating, and all things we do to let ourselves (and others) off the hook. The prophet, on the other hand, is intent on amplifying responsibility and is impatient with excuses. He will not give sin a pass, so his words are often designed to shock rather than to edify. He tries to shake people out of their business-as-usual complacency:[7]

> Tremble, you women who are at ease, shudder, you complacent ones; strip, and make yourself bare, and tie sackcloth around your waist. (Isa 32:11 ESV)

5. Heschel, *Prophets*, 17.
6. Heschel, *Prophets*, 5.
7. Heschel, *Prophets*, 8.

Perhaps we can forgive the prophets for engaging in hyperbole and generalizations in their rhetoric. Here's an example from Jeremiah:

> Run to and fro through the streets of Jerusalem, look and take note! Search her squares to see if you can find a man, one who does justice and seeks truth, . . . For from the least to the greatest of them, everyone is greedy for unjust gain; and from the prophet to the priest, everyone deals falsely. (Jer 5:1; 6:13 ESV)

These are overstatements. But Jeremiah's concern is not with factual accuracy, but with the meaning of the facts. His rhetorical extravagance concerns the significance of human deeds that "cannot be expressed by statistics . . .What seems to be exaggeration is often only a deeper penetration, for the prophets see the world from the point of view of God, as transcendent, not immanent, truth."[8]

The prophets know that religion can distort what the Lord demands of man (Mic 6:8) and that priests themselves had committed perjury by bearing false witness, condoning such sins as violence . . . deceit instead of calling out these sins.[9] In other words, religious leaders had often been part of the problem.

Jeremiah calls Israel's religious piety as fraud and illusion. Worship accompanied by oppression, stealing, idolatry and other evils makes no sense. God's sanctuary is doomed when people indulge in unholy deeds (Jer 7:1-15).[10]

The prophet seems to be an iconoclast, challenging time-honored and cherished beliefs.[11] He is an against-the-grain type of person—the person in the crowd who will stand out for his outside-the-box thinking. He could be called a dissident—certainly not the type who simply goes along with the crowd. He will not buckle to public opinion. He's not afraid to challenge the status

---

8. Heschel, *Prophets*, 15–17.
9. Heschel, *Prophets*, 13.
10. Heschel, *Prophets*, 13.
11. Heschel, *Prophets*, 12.

quo. Jeremiah, for example, must have come across as blasphemous when he said:

> What use to me is frankincense that comes from Sheba, or sweet cane from a distant land? Your burnt offerings are not acceptable, nor your sacrifices pleasing to me. (Jer 6:20 ESV)

Despite the railing against oppression and idolatry, prophets were sometimes palpably affected by their messages of judgment and felt anguish by their own messages from God. They could be disturbed, terrified, and bewildered, even when the messages were being delivered to *Israel's enemies*. Listen to Isaiah's distressing words when he has to prophesy against Babylon:

> At this my body is racked with pain, pangs seize me, like those of a woman in labor; I am staggered by what I hear, I am bewildered by what I see. My heart falters, fear makes me tremble; the twilight I longed for has become a horror to me. (Isa 21:3–4 NIV)

IS THERE A PROPHETIC PERSONALITY?

With all these ideas swirling around, can we say that there is there such a thing as a prophetic personality or prophetic bent? First of all, I am not going to cite any empirical studies that have actually looked at this. There may be some; I just don't know. But it would be extremely difficult, I would think, to collect data and draw definitive conclusions about this. However, I believe it is fair to say that God would not completely override someone's personality when sending them on a prophetic task. In other words, the prophets probably already had an iconoclastic or dissident streak in them when they received their prophetic call.

Certainly, God can use anyone for any kind of task. He used the "foremost" of sinners (1 Tim 1:15, ESV) to become apostle to the Gentiles. However, it's hard to see a "Mary Sunshine" or someone with a Pollyanna-type disposition called to do the heavy lifting demanded in prophetic ministry. Can you imagine a person who always looks on the bright side of things delivering doom-and-gloom messages to people who don't want to hear? I think Heschel would agree because he states, "The prophets do not become absorbed into God, losing their own personalities, but share the divine pathos through their own sharply honed sympathy . . . the prophets' own emotional experiences actively color their fellowship with the divine consciousness and their transmission of God's message."[12] In addition, when God gave us his inspired written Word through the Holy Spirit and through human authors, he did not override their human personalities; the individual books of Scripture have the styles and traits of their human authors.

In short, what I have aimed at is an understanding of what it means to think, feel, respond, and act as a prophet. Although it's impossible to actually grasp exactly what their consciousness was like, I think we have some idea of what stirred the prophet—of what moved them at particular moments in time. First of all, it's clear they saw things from God's point of view, not man's. They brought the world into divine focus. It's not that they were merely miffed or offended by the moral state of affairs; their indignation was from a divine perspective. This gets us in the right direction in understanding their thinking and passion. They were called by God to a task. This sense of calling is, I think, key in understanding their motivation, perspective, and passion.

WHERE DO I FIT IN?

Where do I fit in to all this? It's a fair question and one I have asked myself over and over. The first question is whether I have that iconoclastic or dissident-type streak that God could work with. Was I born with a prophetic personality? Well, I don't know if I was born with one, but a certain dissident or iconoclastic bent came out in me in the mid-1990s when I was employed by a hospital as their medical director for a primary care facility. As I became aware of considerable failings and lapses in patient care, I went to the CEO

---

12. Heschel, *Prophets*, xv–xvi.

of the hospital with my concerns. They were ignored. As poor logistical support from the hospital continued, leading to depletion of medical supplies, and poorly trained support staff and other issues were ignored—all jeopardizing and possibly endangering patient care—I had had enough. So, I got the written support of concerned doctors and nurses and wrote a letter to the board of directors. Our concerns were both clinical and ethical. I would not take the pressure off. So, as things turned out, I became the perceived gang leader and whistleblower in the workplace standing up to an entire hospital power structure. Not surprisingly, my contract was wrongfully terminated. I could have sued the hospital, which I was advised not to do because they had all the powerful attorneys and the deep pockets. I had neither. I suppose you could say that in some ways I lost because my family and I suffered financially for over a year. The money doesn't matter—what matters is right and wrong. What I do have is a clear conscience. In the end, I won because I was on the right side of truth.

In the next chapter, I will describe a situation when Elaine and I left our mainline church and started attending another church where we heard the testimony of a fraud. Because of my prior experience in the workplace, I already had something God could work with, something God could mold into prophetic indignation and passion. God could get me to see things his way. He could enable me to stand up to power structures with the truth.

11

MY PROPHETIC TASK

> There may be times when we are powerless to prevent injustice, but there must never be a time when we fail to protest.
> —Elie Wiesel

A PASTOR AND HIS CON MAN

THE NARRATIVE CONTEXT FOR my prophetic calling and task begins when Elaine and I were attending a church where we heard the amazing testimony of a man who was at death's doorstep with a serious chronic medical condition and who had a dramatic healing he attributed to a super diet that cured him. This led to his bestselling book in which he claims that this revolutionary diet was inspired by God. Now, we had been invited to this church previously by a friend of mine who sold me on its evangelical merits. Elaine and I had previously attended a mainline church that we perceived was growing stale and dull to the gospel message.

Anyway, when we heard this amazing testimony, the person giving the testimony had decided to tell the world of his astonishing healing and his so-called gospel of wellness by marketing a line of dietary and nutritional products. He did this by forging a connection between his healing and his products. His company heavily targeted a marketer's paradise of trusting evangelical souls, reaping a heavenly tens of millions of dollars in annual sales.

The problem? His marketing was a scam and his products snake oil. He and his company were engaged in fraudulent marketing of its products and were in serious trouble with the Food and Drug Administration. Somehow he failed to mention this when he shared his God-honoring testimony. Nevertheless, his marketing juggernaut was cashing in by shamelessly exploiting the church through weaving his wellness gospel seamlessly into the larger prosperity message within the larger evangelical subculture through the skillful use of commonsense nutritional advice, wildly out-of-context Bible verses, clever biblical imagery, and pseudo-scientific mumbo jumbo—all aimed at selling his products.

I became aware of this odious marketing scam rather providentially, but once I discovered the details I became outraged and repulsed that a professed Christian was using God to serve mammon. He was fleecing the people of God and ripping off God's elect by co-opting the sacred faith handed down once for all to the saints (Jude 1:3) in service to his money-grubbing business interests. I saw the entire thing as a stench in God's nostrils (Amos 4:10b).

So, I decided the tables needed to be turned on this intolerable situation. I went to the pastor of the church and provided him clear and copious documentation of fraudulent misrepresentations, with the understanding that as a minister of the gospel he would do the right thing. It was also my assumption that our pastor did not know of the scam when he gave his member a glowing thumbs-up endorsement in the author's book, praising his "great integrity." However, now that he was aware of the deceit, he should at least come clean with his congregation and admit he himself had made a mistake, especially since he had stood arm-in-arm with this slick opportunist when he had given a God-honoring, but wantonly hypocritical, testimony in church.

To make the situation a lot messier, the authors's academic credentials, which he used to claim expert status in selling his modern-day snake oil, were fake—totally bogus. For example, he claimed a PhD in nutrition from a school (degree mill) that didn't even offer that degree. I guess he believed in miracles, because he claimed to have a degree that didn't even exist!

My guiding principle was simple: God "detests dishonest scales" (Prov 11:1a ESV). In other words, God cares deeply about how business affairs are conducted—about buying and selling. "Dishonest scales" refers to cheating people. God loathes deception of any kind when it comes to business transactions. The Old Testament prophets constantly railed against economic injustice, including dishonest business practices. Ministers of the gospel should care no less about these things.

However, our pastor's response threw ice-cold water on my expectations. Instead of biblically (graciously) confronting and disciplining a member of his flock who was committing public sin (swindling) in conformity to 1 Corinthians 5, he took a head-in-the-sand approach that refused to look at unpalatable facts objectively. He said his church was doing a lot of good things for God and had had lots of decisions for Christ—those kinds of things. So, he believed that all we needed to do was to pray and "leave the situation in God's hands." Even though he did talk with the person of interest, he chose to believe the story of an opportunist and deceiver rather than the facts, which showed direct evidence of fraud and wrongdoing.

However, I reminded him although that I was glad that the church was doing lots of good things for God and that prayer and trust in God are good, in this situation they appeared to be a game plan for losers because they were a pious excuse from exercising any kind of meaningful moral action. I don't see the apostle Paul doing this in 1 Corinthians 5—he took action.

CONTEMPORARY PROPHETIC OUTRAGE— PROPHET MOTIVE CONFRONTS PROFIT MOTIVE

When a Christian businessman gives a testimony that honors God, all the time concealing his crooked marketing and phony degrees, I would say that most of us would be outraged at the shameless hypocrisy and brazen contempt for God and his people. The outrage only gets worse when his pastor sticks to his guns and continues praising his member's "great integrity."

The pastor's response—or non-response—kindled a prophetic-like burning in my heart. When a church member used God to serve mammon by wanton deception in the church and shamelessly twisted some of the most sublime passages in Holy Scripture into a cheap marketing tool, my sense of injustice reached almost cosmic proportions. I began sensing that God had sent me to that church to engage in prophetic ministry—evil had to be confronted. God's people were being fleeced by a con man, and it seemed nobody in the church either knew about it or seemed to care, although it was well known online that he was a charlatan. Christ's church was being harmed. A deceiver was at large in the church and his pastor complicit. This was not business as usual, so the walls of this situation had to come tumbling down with the truth.

Using God's holy Word to market sleazy products amounted to reducing Scripture to mere slogans to manipulate people to buy. Such vulgar debasement of God's Word (For example, the Prologue of John's Gospel was contorted beyond belief and used as marketing verses! The apostle whom Jesus loved must have been rolling over in his grave in holy disgust.), which is intended to bring us to salvation and communion with God, not to sell merchandise, was too much for me. I considered this situation an epic pastoral failure. The pastor wouldn't budge, so I decided to go elsewhere.

Through a contact in Texas, I was led to a journalist with a national newspaper who had a mutual interest in "congregations being well served by their pastors." She was interested in doing a piece on our pastor and his con man but, at the last minute, bailed out and did a less threatening article on charlatans in general.

In the meantime, I tried to block publication of his soon-to-be-published book with a major Christian publishing house, even going to the CEO—all to no avail. It seemed to me that the publisher was more interested in publishing than ethics.

The author, for his part, got wind of my efforts to stop his marketing and publishing scam, and he threatened legal action against me for making false, defamatory, libelous, and slanderous statements against him in an effort to discredit him. For my part, I had to hire legal representation to protect myself against possible litigation, which never came to pass. So, on went his publishing and sleazy merchandising, all in God's name.

GOD HAS THE LAST WORD

I have to say that I was willing to go to the mat in pursuit of justice and truth. I would have sacrificed my career and finances to expose what I perceived was an evil influence in the midst of the church. However, I was not able to prevail against the earthly powers aligned against me.

But as I read the Old Testament prophets, they, too, often did not prevail here on earth. Their messages were ignored, and they were often persecuted and killed. But they were faithful to God's calling to deliver a message.

Listen to Isaiah's harsh rebuke of God's people who wanted to hear "pleasant things" rather than the truth:

> Go now, write it on a tablet for them, inscribe it on a scroll, that for the days to come it may be an everlasting witness. For these are . . . children unwilling to listen to the Lord's instruction. They say to the seers, "See no more visions!" and to the prophets, "Give us no more visions of what is right! Tell us pleasant things, prophesy illusions. Leave this way, get off this path, and stop confronting us with the Holy One of Israel!" (Isa 30:8–11 NIV)

I delivered a message that was ignored by people and Christian institutions in power. However, I have a clear conscience before God that I did the right thing and delivered the right message.

In the end, though, God always has the last word. His grace is always available. Hear the end of Isaiah's oracle in which God wants to show lovingkindness to his stubborn people:

Yet the Lord longs to be gracious to you; therefore he will rise up to show you compassion. For the Lord is a God of justice. Blessed are all who wait for him! (Isa 30:18 NIV)

We all need God's grace—myself included. I have failed to listen to God many times, so I pray for those in ministry and leadership positions who may have failed to listen when they should have.

I have to believe the words of one of Job's friends, in a celebration of the goodness of God:

> He performs wonders that cannot be fathomed, miracles that cannot be counted . . . He thwarts the plans of the crafty, so that their hands achieve no success. He catches the wise in their craftiness, and the schemes of the wily are swept away. Darkness comes upon them in the daytime; at noon they grope as in the night . . . and injustice shuts its mouth. (Job 5:9–16 NIV)

EPILOGUE

I have been young, and now am old, yet I have not seen the righteous forsaken, or his sons begging for bread. (Ps 37:25 ESV)

FOUR DECADES AGO, ELAINE and I were young when I had the two prophetic visions. Our faith journey from Guadalajara to Miami was exhilarating. We are now growing old and our health failing. In the intervening years we have raised five children and now have ten grandchildren. I have had a long career in medicine, and Elaine and I have had the privilege of serving some of the poorest people on earth as medical missionaries to the Congo (then Zaïre) for three years.

However, my prophetic experience has been etched into my soul forever. It's like God has branded me as his eternal possession. On occasion, tears still well up in me when I recall what the Lord did for Elaine and and me—it was that kind of experience. Eternal gratitude is mine for a compassionate God who has stooped down to Elaine and me and shown us his mighty hand. I don't necessarily think that everyone will have the same kind of supernatural experience we had, especially in our Western culture. But it is my hope that more believers can learn to see their lives within some kind of biblical pattern or narrative.

I firmly believe that God continues to work according to his ordained types and patterns in the lives of believers today. But we have to be alert to such patterns, and we have to know Scripture, especially its overall narrative. I think too many of us still read the Bible in a piecemeal fashion, not really getting its overall plot structure.[1] This needs to be corrected.

Nancy Guthrie's wonderful book *Even Better than Eden: Nine Ways the Bible's Story Changes Everything about Your Story*[2] would be a good place to start. She's a terrific writer, and her book is tailor-made for small group studies to help us understand how our stories fit in to the grand stories of Scripture. Seeing our life stories fitting in with the narratives of Scripture will strengthen our faith. Her book will help you.

One biblical pattern I have not mentioned and have saved for last is the pattern of humbling and exaltation—the reversal of one's fortunes. This needs explanation.

Listen to the beautiful verses given to us the week before classes were to begin at the University of Miami, when Elaine and I were eagerly anticipating meeting with Ms. Binns after Labor Day:

> Humble yourselves, therefore, under the mighty hand of God, *that he may exalt* you at the proper time . . . your adversary, the devil, prowls about like a roaring lion seeking someone to devour. But resist him, firm in your faith. (1 Pet 5:6–9 TEV, italics added)

During the time of our experience four decades ago, Elaine and I were constantly filling our hearts with songs of praise, very often related to humbling ourselves, e.g.: "If you want to be great in God's kingdom learn to be the servant of all," and "Humble thyselves in the sight of the Lord, and he will lift you up."

The verses in 1 Peter contain a wonderful promise of exaltation. Humbling and exaltation are prominent themes interwoven in the biblical narrative. I like to say that God is a God of reversals. There are many reversals in the biblical record. One reversal will occur on the Day of the Lord, when the wicked and arrogant are punished and the righteous rewarded.

---

1. See Lubeck, *Reading the Bible for a Change*.
2. Guthrie, *Even Better than Eden*.

EPILOGUE

I think you know how much I love the book of Isaiah; he is a masterful poet whose lofty prose and poetry are richly layered and saturated with God's Word. Let's hear what he says about a complete reversal and utter transformation of our current perverted society in the eschatological future:

> See, a king will reign in righteousness . . . and a refuge from the storm, like streams of water in the desert . . . No longer will the fool be called noble nor the scoundrel be highly respected. For fools speak folly, their hearts are bent on evil: They practice ungodliness and spread error concerning the Lord; the hungry they leave empty and from the thirsty they withhold water. Scoundrels use wicked methods, they make up evil schemes to destroy the poor with lies, even when the plea of the needy is just. But the noble make noble plans, and by noble deeds they stand. (Isa 32:1–8 NIV)

The late Russian dissident, Nobel laureate, and titanic moral figure Aleksandr Solzhenitsyn gave what I think is one of the best critiques ever of Western decadence in his 1978 Harvard commencement address. His was a courageous, no-holds-barred dose of "Veritas" (Harvard's motto). This was the day Harvard went to school, when Western spiritual exhaustion and godless Western self-congratulatory smugness were unapologetically unmasked. The speech was not especially well received by the intelligentsia.[3] (Reminds me of Isaiah 30:10a NIV: "Give us no more visions of what's right!")

Mankind has failed miserably and repeatedly in its attempts to bring about the perfect society, only causing misery on top of more misery. But it won't be long before utopia and paradise will be ushered in by the King of righteousness. What a glorious day that will be!

---

3. Solzhenitsyn's commencement address, "A World Split Apart," can be read in its entirety, along with twelve early responses and six later reflections in Berman, ed., *Solzhenitsyn at Harvard*.

The ultimate reversal, of course, will be the exaltation of our Lord Jesus Christ, who for the shame that he suffered will be crowned Lord of lords and King of kings. God does the exalting.

OTHER REVERSALS IN SCRIPTURE

There are, of course, many other reversals in the biblical record. Who can forget how Joseph was ditched by his brothers, sold into slavery, but exalted by God into prominence in the Egyptian government. How about Daniel and his three friends, who were repeatedly tested but refused to compromise and give in to pagan kings and were rewarded by God and exalted to prominence through the agency of wicked men.

However, my favorite reversal in Scripture is found the Old Testament narrative of 1 Samuel 2:1–10, which records the beautiful prayer of Hannah. I love her prayer, which records her praise of the God who exalts the humble and humbles the proud and arrogant. This was after she had been mercilessly taunted and provoked by her rival, Peninnah, for being childless. But God remembered Hannah and gave her Samuel, whom she dedicated to the Lord. Her prayer is a beautiful reminder of how God works in the world:

> The Lord makes poor and makes rich; he brings low and he exalts. He raises up the poor from the dust; he lifts the needy from the ash heap to make the poor sit with princes and inherit a seat of honor. (1 Sam 2:7–8a ESV)

The weak, infertile, and unimpressive are exalted. The high and mighty, handsome and powerful, are brought down by God. The Bible makes important distinctions between those who rely on their own strength and resources and those who rely on God. Hannah, in her distress, prayed to God for a son, and he remembered her with one of the most godly men in Scripture.

David certainly saw his victories as coming from God. He trusted in God to give him victory over his enemies. Despite being a man of war, David did not hesitate to call upon the name of the Lord. Read his Song of Deliverance and last words in 2 Samuel

EPILOGUE

22:1—23:7. You will be impressed by the richness of the words and the beauty of David's love for God.

Let's not forget the words of our Savior, who said in Matthew 23:12:

> Whoever exalts himself will be humbled, and whoever humbles himself will be exalted. (ESV)

We humble ourselves and put our trust in the Lord. God does the exalting. Reversals are his business.

I would like to close out this book with a dramatic reversal story that occurred while Elaine and I were missionaries in Africa. It involves a little girl and a disease that could have killed her.

ONE FINAL STORY

A LITTLE MISSIONARY GIRL AND MALARIA

IN SEPTEMBER 1988, ELAINE and I were medical missionaries in Zaïre (now the Democratic Republic of the Congo) Africa. We had one daughter, Kendra, who was four years old. We came back to the States (Daytona Beach, Florida) in early September so Elaine could deliver our second child, a boy, in early November. Everything was fine until Kendra began running fevers.

One evening I had taken her to see the movie *Bambi*, but we had to leave early because she said, "Daddy, my bones hurt." Elaine and I had previously taken Kendra to see her pediatrician, who thought she most likely had a viral infection.

The next day we were in Orlando (actually Oviedo) and stopped at a local Wendy's to grab a bite to eat. I stayed in the car while Elaine and Kendy went inside to order. Then events started to turn tragic very quickly. While I sat in the car waiting for Elaine and Kendy, a lady knocked on my window and told me that my daughter was "having problems walking."

Elaine was sitting on the curb outside the restaurant holding Kendra in her arms, so I quickly got out of the car, picked Kendy up, and we drove (actually sped) to Halifax Hospital in Daytona Beach, where I had previously done my residency in family medicine. On our way there, Kendra went into a coma. In a panic, all we could say was, "Help us, Jesus!!"

ONE FINAL STORY

When we arrived in the emergency room, Kendra was still in a coma and had a fever of 106 degrees F. Her pupils were sluggish, and she showed signs of brain damage. A malaria blood test showed that her little body was overwhelmed with malaria. (For you medical people, her malaria smear showed 37 percent parasitemia—unbelievably high.) Kendy had roughly a 60–70 percent chance of dying. Elaine and I were devastated.

The emergency room doctors quickly arranged to have Kendra helicoptered to Shands Hospital at the University of Florida in Gainesville. I will never forget the terribly empty feelings Elaine and I had as we saw our little daughter loaded into the chopper and flown off. We hastily drove that night, September 15, to Gainesville, panic-stricken, not knowing if we would ever see Kendra again. Our fear was that she would be dead when we arrived at Shands.

Well, she was not dead, but still in a coma—critically ill. Her doctor, Dr. Ayoub, was very kind and understanding but pulled no punches: her chances of recovery were not good. She had severe cerebral malaria.[1] We were in a state of shock for almost two days—really struggling emotionally and spiritually. But we started to get ourselves together. Our first step was to realize that Kendra ultimately did not belong to us, but to God, and was given to us as parents to raise in a godly way. Therefore, we put our little girl in God's loving hands. We put our trust in him. This was very hard for us, because parents instinctively have a hard time letting their children go.

---

1. Malaria is a parasitic infection transmitted to humans by mosquito bites by the *Anopheles* mosquito and is found throughout the tropics. In someone who has no or little immunity it can be devastating because it can affect almost any part of the body, with failure of almost any or all organ systems. Cerebral malaria, which Kendra had, involves the brain, with brain edema (swelling), and can lead to impaired consciousness, seizures, coma, and death. With treatment, mortality is 15–20 percent, although we were told in Kendra's case it was much higher. About 15 percent of children survivors of cerebral malaria have complications, including cerebral palsy, paralysis on one side of the body, deafness, blindness, epilepsy, and language and mental deficits. Source: UpToDate last updated March 17, 2022 Wolters Kluwer 3.50.3 2011–2022.

Our immediate families were distressed. The situation looked hopeless—but we came together for Kendra. I will never forget praying for Kendy in the hospital chapel with Elaine's two sisters, Eileen and Elinda. All four of us were in tears.

Elaine and I were graciously given a nice place to stay in the Ronald McDonald House next to the hospital. However, I felt an overwhelming need to be alone and go before the living God and intercede for our little girl. So I checked in to the Bambi Motel (what a coincidence), where I knelt beside the bed, tears flowing down my cheeks, and—my heart broken—pleaded with God to heal little Kendra. It was a prayer of desperation.

God heard our prayers and led us to Bible verses that spoke to us in a time of great need, For example, Deuteronomy 12:5–7 speaks of giving the firstborn as a sacrifice to God, something we had already decided to do in a spiritual way, although the comparison cannot be stretched too far because the Old Testament text refers to animal sacrifices. But at that time the verses spoke to me in our situation.[2] I knew we were at least doing something right in a spiritual sense.

I also went back to 1 Samuel 30, where David was also in a desperate situation—he was in danger of being killed by his own men. So, he went before the Lord, who promised complete restoration. Reading this story again (see our testimony in chapter 2), the Holy Spirit spoke to me and, I believe, told me that Kendra would be completely restored.

While Kendy was comatose in the PICU (Pediatric Intensive Care Unit), Elaine and I took turns being at her bedside—I had the night shift. What precious moments we had. I vividly remember singing to our little girl about Jesus while gently combing my fingers through her hair. I don't know if she heard me, but Jesus did.

---

2. In the Old Testament all firstborn creatures belong to God, human and animal. After the golden calf incident, the Levites took the place of the firstborn in Israel (Exod 32:25–29). The principle that all the firstborn belong to God goes all the way back to the exodus—the tenth plague, when all the firstborn Israelites had to be consecrated to God (Exod 11:4—13:15) See Wenham, *Numbers*, 80.

On the third and forth days of Kendra's coma, God began giving me a supernatural peace—one that passes all understanding (Phil 4:7). I had an overwhelming assurance that Kendra was going to be restored, even though she was still in a coma. This kind of assurance and peace from God was a beautiful experience.

So, I told Elaine that I knew God was going to restore Kendy and that we were going back to Zaïre after Kyle David was born.[3] This was on a Sunday morning, September 18. Therefore, I left the hospital and went to the mall at Gainesville to buy some much-needed clothes for our return to Africa. Shortly after returning to the PICU, a nurse came to the waiting room and told me, "Mr. Fisher, your daughter is waking up and starting to talk." Wow!

It would be hard to put into words the joy Elaine and I had in that moment. Three days later Kendra was discharged—totally restored.

This experience has never left out hearts. God was gracious and merciful. It also affected a little girl. For example, before returning to Zaïre, I was driving Kendra to preschool. On the way there we stopped at a local Burger King. As we were pulling out of the drive-thru, I noticed Kendra writing something on her tablet. My curiosity sparked, I asked her, "What are you writing, Kendy?" She responded, "Daddy, I'm writing a letter to Jesus. 'Dear Jesus, thank you for healing my body.'"

Two years later, when we were living in the Boston area and attending a large regional church, Kendra had the courage to stand up in front of a large congregation and tell how God had

---

3. Kyle was born November 4, 1988, in Daytona Beach, Florida, the same day that Kendra had her six-week follow-up visit in Gainesville with Dr. Ayoub. Kyle was our promised son. The Bible has many stories of barren women who were promised children by God. We can think of Sarah, Hannah, and Elizabeth, mother of John the Baptist. When we were in Zaïre, Elaine had problems conceiving for over a year, so we made it a matter of prayer before the Lord. God led us to the story in 2 Kings 4 of the Shunammite woman. She was barren and her husband old. Elisha told her, "At this season, about this time next year, you shall embrace a son" (v. 16a ESV). Well . . . we took this as a word from God that Elaine would have a boy next year. Wouldn't you know it . . . she conceived, and Kyle David was born the following year—our child of promise.

miraculously healed her of malaria. Elaine and I could not have more proud of her.

More importantly, we thank a great and merciful God for reversing what started out as a tragedy into a victory. Kendra is living proof and a celebration for what the living God can do in our lives. To him be the glory forever!

FIGURE 3

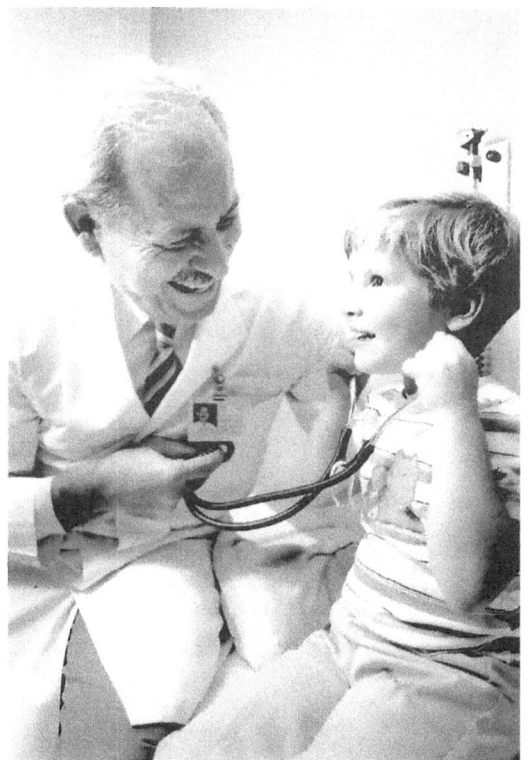

Kendra with Dr. Ayoub at her six-week follow-up clinic visit at the University of Florida Clinic. Our first son, Kyle, was born earlier that morning, November 4, 1988.

Bibliography

Alexander, T. Desmond. *City of God and the Goal of Creation*. Wheaton, IL: Crossway, 2018.

———. *From Eden to the New Jerusalem: An Introduction to Biblical Theology*. Grand Rapids: Kregel Academic, 2008.

Anselm. *Prayers and Meditations of St. Anselm with the Proslogion*. Translated by Bendicta Ward. New York: Penguin Classics, 1973.

Arnold, Clinton E. *3 Crucial Questions about Spiritual Warfare*. Grand Rapids: Baker Academic, 1997.

Bates, Matthew W. *Gospel Allegiance*. Grand Rapids: Brazos, 2019.

———. *The Gospel Precisely: Surprisingly Good News about Jesus Christ the King*. Middletown, DE: Renew Resource, 2021.

———. *What Faith in Jesus Misses for Salvation in Christ*. Grand Rapids: Brazos, 2019.

Beale, G. K. *The Temple in the Church's Mission: A Biblical Theology of the Dwelling Place of God*. NSBT 17. Downers Grove, IL: InterVarsity, 2004.

Beilby, James K., and Paul Rhodes, eds. *Understanding Spiritual Warfare: Four Views*. Grand Rapids: Baker Academic, 2012.

Berman, Ronald, ed. *Solzhenitsyn at Harvard: The Addresses, Twelve Early Responses and Six Later Reflections*. Washington, DC: Ethics and Public Policy Center, 1980.

Boersma, Hans. *Heavenly Participation: The Weaving of a Sacramental Tapestry*. Grand Rapids: Eerdmans, 2011.

———. *Seeing God: The Beatific Vision in Christian Tradition*. Grand Rapids: Eerdmans, 2018.

Boyd, Gregory A. *God at War: The Biblical & Spiritual Conflict*. Downers Grove, IL: IVP Academic 1997.

Bright, John. *The Kingdom of God: The Biblical Concept and Its Meaning for the Church*. Nashville: Abington, 1981.

Brown, Michael L. *Authentic Fire: A Response to John MacArthur's Strange Fire*. Lake Mary, FL: Creation House, 2015.

Bruce, F. F. *The Books of Acts*. NICOT. Grand Rapids: Eerdmans, 1988.

Burgis, Tom. *Kleptopia: How Dirty Money Is Conquering the World*. New York: Harper Collins, 2020.

Clowney, E. P. "The Final Temple." *Westminster Theological Journal* 35 (1973) 184–85.

Collins, John, J. *Daniel: A Commentary on the Book of Daniel*. Hermeneia, Minneapolis: Fortress, 1993.

Cook, William F., III, and Chuck Lawless. *Spiritual Warfare in the Storyline of Scripture: A Biblical, Theological and Practical Approach*. Nashville: B&H Academic, 2019.

Deere, Jack. *Surprised by the Voice of God: How God Speaks Today through Prophecies, Dreams, and Visions*. Grand Rapids: Zondervan, 1996.

Edgar, William. *Created and Creating: A Biblical Theology of Culture*. Downers Grover, IL: IVP Academic, 2017.

Estelle, Brian D. *Echoes of Exodus: Tracing a Biblical Motif*. Downers Grove, IL: IVP Academic, 2018.

Gentry, Peter J., and Stephen J. Wellum. *Kingdom through Covenant: A Biblical-Theological Understanding of the Covenants*. Wheaton, IL: Crossway, 2015.

Goldingay, John. *Daniel*. WBC, Dallas: Word, 1989.

Grudem, Wayne. *Systematic Theology: An Introduction to Biblical Doctrine*. Grand Rapids: Zondervan, 1994.

Guthrie, Nancy. *Even Better than Eden: Nine Ways the Bible's Story Changes Everything about Your Story*. Wheaton, IL: Crossway, 2018.

Habermas, Gary. Review of *Kingdom Triangle: Recover the Christian Mind, Renovate the Soul, Restore the Spirit's Power* by J. P. Moreland. *Philosophia Christi* 11:1 (2009) 215–23. Hamilton, James M., Jr. *What Is Biblical Theology?: Guide to the Bible's Story, Symbolism, and Patterns*. Wheaton, IL: Crossway, 2014.

———. *With the Clouds of Heaven: The Book of Daniel in Biblical Theology*. NSBT 32. Downers Grove, IL: InterVarsity, 2014.

Heschel, Abraham J. *The Prophets*. New York: Harper Perennial Modern Classics, 1962.

Hoekema, Anthony A. *The Bible and the Future*. Grand Rapids: Eerdmans, 1979.

Horton, Michael Scott, ed. *Power Religion: The Selling Out of the Evangelical Church?* Chicago: Moody, 1992.

Keener, Craig S. *Miracles Today: The Supernatural Work of God in the Modern World*. Grand Rapids: Baker Academic, 2021.

Kelly, Douglas F. *Systematic Theology*. Vol. 1, *The God Who Is: The Holy Trinity*. Ross-shire, Scotland: Mentor Imprint, Christian Focus, 2008.

Kimbrough, S. T., Jr. *Partakers of the Divine Life: Participation in the Divine Nature in the Writings of Charles Wesley*. Eugene, OR: Cascade, 2016.

Kraft, Charles H. *Christianity with Power: Your Worldview and Your Experience of the Supernatural*. Eugene, OR: Wipf & Stock, 1989.

Ladd, George Eldon. *A Theology of the New Testament*. Grand Rapids: Eerdmans, 1974.

———. *The Gospel of the Kingdom: Scriptural Studies in the Kingdom of God*. Grand Rapids: Eerdmans: 1959.

BIBLIOGRAPHY

———. *New Testament and Criticism*. Grand Rapids: Eerdmans, 1967.
Lakoff, George, and Mark Johnson. *Metaphors We Live By*. Chicago: University of Chicago Press, 2003.
Lewis, C. S. *Perelandra*. New York: Scribner, 1944.
———. *Screwtape Letters*. New York: Harper, 1942.
Lubeck, Ray. *Reading the Bible for a Change: Understanding and Responding to God's Word*. 2nd ed. Eugene, OR: Wipf & Stock, 2023.
MacArthur, John. *Strange Fire: Danger of Offending the Holy Spirit with Counterfeit Worship*. Nashville: Thomas Nelson, 2013.
Martin, Oren. *Bound for the Promised Land: The Land in God's Redemptive Plan*. NSBT 34. Downers Grove, IL: InterVarsity, 2015.
McKnight, Scott. *King Jesus Gospel: The Original Good News Revisited*. Grand Rapids: Zondervan, 2016.
Meyer, Jason C. *Progressive Covenantalism: Charting a Course Between Dispensational and Covenant Theologies*. Nashville: B&H Academic, 2016.
Middleton, Richard J. *A New Heaven and a New Earth: Reclaiming Biblical Eschatology*. Grand Rapids: Baker Academic, 2014.
Moreland, J. P. *Kingdom Triangle: Recover the Christian Mind, Renovate the Soul, Restore the Spirit's Power*. Grand Rapids: Zondervan, 2007.
Morphew, Derek. *Breakthrough: Discovering the Kingdom*. Cape Town, South Africa: Vineyard International Publishing, 1991.
Mouw, Richard J. *When the Kings Come Marching In: Isaiah and the New Jerusalem*. Grand Rapids: Eerdmans, 2002.
Oswalt, John N. *The Book of Isaiah: Chapters 1–39*. NICOT. Grand Rapids: Eerdmans, 1986.
Robertson, O. Palmer. *Christ of Wisdom: A Redemptive-Historical Exploration of the Wisdom Books of the Old Testament*. Philipsburg: P&R, 2017.
Rutven, Jon Mark. *On the Cessation of the Charismata: The Protestant Polemic on Post-Biblical Miracles*. Tulsa: Word & Spirit Press, 2011.
Sandy, D. Brent. *Plowshares & Pruning Hooks: Rethinking the Language of Biblical Prophecy and Apocalyptic*. Downers Grove, IL: IVP Academic, 2002.
Sherman, Dean, with Bill Payne. *Spiritual Warfare for Every Christian: How to Live in Victory and Retake the Land*. Seattle, WA: YWAM, 1990.
Smith, James K. A. *How (Not) to Be Secular: Reading Charles Taylor*. Grand Rapids: Eerdmans, 2014.
Waymeyer, Matt. *Amillennialism and the Age to Come: A Premillennial Critique of the Two-Age Model*. Kress Biblical Resources, 2016.
Wenham, Gordon J. *Numbers*. TOTC 4. Downers Grove, IL: IVP Academic, 1981.
White, Tom. *The Believer's Guide to Spiritual Warfare*. Grand Rapids: Chosen Books, 2011.
Willard, Dallas. *The Great Omission: Reclaiming Jesus's Essential Teachings on Discipleship*. New York: HarperOne, 2006.

BIBLIOGRAPHY

Wink, Walter. *Engaging the Powers: Discernment and Resistance in a World of Domination.* Minneapolis, MN: Fortress, 1992.

———. *Naming the Powers: The Language of Power in the New Testament.* Minneapolis, MN: Fortress, 1984.

———. *Unmasking the Powers: The Invisible Powers that Determine Human Existence.* Minneapolis, MN: Fortress, 1986.

Index

OLD TESTAMENT

Genesis

	81n15, 82, 86
1	85n27
1–2	84
1:9 ESV	85
1:12 ESV	85
1:18 ESV	83, 85
1:21 ESV	85
1:25 ESV	85
1:26–28	83, 84, 84n27, 85n27
1:27	82
1:28	82
1:31 ESV	85
2	82
2:15	81n15, 84
12:1	59
12:2–3	58
12:4	59
12:4a ESV	58
15	58, 59
15:16–18	61

Exodus

3	27n1
3:19 ESV	27n1
3:19–20	27n1
6:1 ESV	27n1
6:1–3	70
11:4—13:15	126n2
13:3	27n1
15	30n5
15:10 ESV	70
19:5 ESV	29
32:11 ESV	27n1
32:25–29	126n2

Numbers

13	10
13:31b–32a KJV	10

Deuteronomy

	27n1, 47
4:34	27n1
5:15	27n1
6:16	64
6:21	27n1
7:6–8 ESV	28
7:8	27n1
7:19	27n1
8:11–18a ESV	xiv
9:26	27n1
10:20–21 ESV	46
11:1–12	47
11:2	27n1
11:2b NIV	47
11:7–8 NIV	47
12:5–7	126
26:3–11	16n1
26:8	27n1

1

INDEX

Joshua
4:23	27n1
4:23–24	27n1

1 Samuel
2:1–10	122
2:7–8a ESV	122
30	126
30:1–8	9

2 Samuel
22:1—23:7	122–123

1 Kings
8:42 ESV	28n1
8:51	28n1

2 Kings
4	127n3
4:16a ESV	127n3
15:29	63n13

2 Chronicles
20:15–17 NASB	11, 28, 38, 74

Job
5:9–16 NIV	117

Psalms
	30, 30n5
8:5–8	84
8:5–8 ESV	83–84
9:1–2	xiv
18:15	31
19:1	94
19:1 ESV	81
19:1–6	33n2
19:7–11	34
19:8a–10 ESV	17
35:27b ESV	22
37:25 ESV	119
77	30n5
77:11–20	30n5
77:13–20	30n5
90:2	52n9
90:4	52n9
110	41
110:1 ESV	42
114	30n5
119:11	34
136:12 ESV	28n1

Proverbs
11:1a ESV	114
16:18a NIV	71

Ecclesiastes
	16n1

Isaiah
	30n6, 61, 62, 63, 66n19, 67, 71, 79, 104, 121
1:1–4 ESV	87–88
2:1 ESV	6n2
5	67
5:1–7	66
7:2	64
7:4	69
7:4 ESV	64
7:7	64
7:9b ESV	64
7:10 ESV	64
7:10–14	64
7–12	62
7–35	62
7–39	61–62
8:7–8 ESV	65
8:11–22	67
9:8—10:4	65
9:8—10:4 ESV	65
9:12b	65

INDEX

9:17b	65	37:38	69, 70
9:21b	65	39:1–8	71
10:4b	65	40–46	66n19
10:5	66	40–55	30n6
10:16–19	66	41:21–24 ESV	72
10:24–34	66	41:21–29	71
10:24b ESV	66	41:25–29	72
11:5–9	79	46:9–10 TLB	10, 72
11:9b ESV	91	46:9b–11 ESV	21
11:10a ESV	19	51:3	22
11:11–16	22	52:13—53:12	79
12	66	54:13	xiv
12:2–5 ESV	66	60	79
12:4b ESV	35	60:1–22	88
13:1—14:23	67	65:17–19a ESV	88
13–27	67	65:17–25	79, 88
13–33	68	66:18–21	88
13–35	63, 67		
21:3–4 NIV	109	**Jeremiah**	
23:1–18	67	5:1 ESV	108
27:2b–3a ESV	67	6:13 ESV	108
27:6b ESV	67	6:20 ESV	109
27:12–13	67	7:1–15	108
27:13 ESV	67	9:23–24 ESV	106
27:13b ESV	67	13:17 ESV	103
30:8–11 NIV	116	31:31	22
30:10a NIV	121	32:20–21	31
30:18 NIV	117		
32:1–8 NIV	121	**Ezekiel**	
32:11 ESV	107	2:5 ESV	104
34	68	3:7–9	104
34–35	68	3:12	34n3
35	68	5:10a ESV	19
35:1–10 ESV	68	8:3	34n3
36:13–20	69	36:35	22
36–39	62, 63, 68		
37:6b ESV	69	**Daniel**	
37:7	69	2:20–22 ESV	72
37:20	69	4:35b ESV	73
37:20b ESV	69	9:15 ESV	27n1, 31
37:26–27 ESV	70	9:23	6n2
37:26–28	70		
37:29b ESV	70		
37:36	70		

3

Hosea

2:15	22
3:5	22
13:16b ESV	19

Joel

2:28	33
3:17–18	80

Amos

1:1	101
1:1 ESV	6n2
4:10b	113
6:4–6 ESV	107
6:8a ESV	106
8:4–6 ESV	105
9:11–15	80

Micah

4:1–5	80
6:8	108

NEW TESTAMENT

Matthew

4:23 NRSV	50
5:8 ESV	93
9:35	50
12:28	51
12:32	52n7
13	49
13:22	95
19:16–25	50
19:23–25	50
23:12 ESV	123
24:14	50
26:13 NRSV	50

Mark

1:15	50, 53
10:17–26	50
10:30	52, 52n7

Luke

10:18 ESV	41
14:26	75n1
16:8	52n7
17:20–21	50
18:18–26	50
22:44 ESV	43
24:25–27 ESV	23

John

	115
4:24	20
6:45	xiv
12:29	xv
12:31	41, 52

Acts

2:17	33
2:32–36	41
7:28 ESV	93
17:11b ESV	xiv
28:31 NRSV	50

Romans

1:20	33n2
7	46
8:14–17	96
8:22–23	54
8:37 ESV	44

1 Corinthians

2:9	97
3:16–17	89
4:20	56
5	114
12:10–11	33

13:12a ESV	98	James		
15:53–54	97	2:22		61

2 Corinthians
3:18a ESV   97

Galatians
1:4   52
4:4–7   96

Ephesians
2:2   43n5
2:7   52n7
6:11–17   43n5
6:12 ESV   39

Philippians
4:7   127

Colossians
2:3 ESV   47
3:1–2   93

1 Thessalonians
4–5   51

2 Thessalonians
          51

1 Timothy
1:15 ESV   109
6:17   52n7

Hebrews
6:5   52n7, 54, 56
6:5 NRSV   49
12:14   96

1 Peter
          44
3:14   10
5:6   28n1
5:6–9 TEV   10–11, 38, 120
5:8 NIV   44

2 Peter
1:3 ESV   97
1:4   94
1:4 ESV   97
1:5–7   97
3:8   52n9

Jude
1:3   113

Revelation
          30, 68
4   22
7:12b ESV   32
11:15   53
11:15 NRSV   51
15:3–4 ESV   32
17:3   34n3
19:11–21   7n3
20:11   7n3
21:1–3 ESV   89
21:3   91
21:3 ESV   90
21:16   90
21:18 ESV   90
21–22   87, 89
22:4   98
22:4 ESV   95
22:4–5 ESV   93

5

EARLY CHRISTIAN WRITINGS

Anselm of Canterbury
  Proslogion   95, 96, 99
Augustine   21, 78n8

GREEK AND ROMAN LITERATURE

Plato   78n8
Plotinus   78n8

www.ingramcontent.com/pod-product-compliance
Lightning Source LLC
Chambersburg PA
CBHW070454100426
42743CB00010B/1619